TEXAS
FRUIT & VEGETABLE GARDENING

TEXAS
FRUIT & VEGETABLE GARDENING

GREG GRANT

Growing Successful Gardeners™

MINNEAPOLIS, MINNESOTA

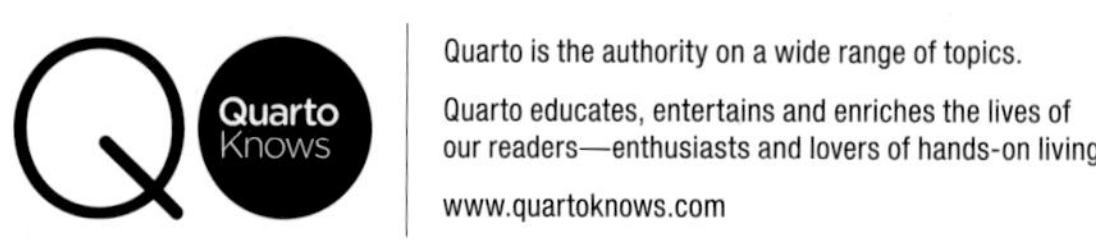

First Published in 2012 by Cool Springs Press, an imprint of Quarto Publishing Group USA Inc., 400 First Avenue North, Suite 400, Minneapolis, MN 55401 USA. Telephone: (612) 344-8100 Fax: (612) 344-8692

quartoknows.com
Visit our blogs at quartoknows.com

Cool Springs Press titles are also available at discounts in bulk quantity for industrial or sales-promotional use. For details write to Special Sales Manager at Cool Springs Press, 400 First Avenue North, Suite 400, Minneapolis, MN 55401 USA.

To find out more about our books, visit us online at www.coolspringspress.com.

ISBN-13: 978-1-59186-531-5

10 9 8 7

Library of Congress Cataloging-in-Publication Data

Grant, Greg, 1939-
Texas fruit & vegetable gardening : plant, grow, and eat the best edibles for Texas gardens / Greg Grant.
p. cm.
Includes index.
ISBN 978-1-59186-531-5 (pbk.)
1. Vegetable gardening--Texas. 2. Fruit-culture--Texas. I. Title. II. Title: Texas fruit and vegetable gardening.

SB321.5.T4G73 2012
635.09764--dc23

2011036099

President/CEO: Ken Fund
Group Publisher: Bryan Trandem
Publisher: Ray Wolf
Senior Editor: Billie Brownell
Editor: Kathy Franz
Creative Director: Michele Lanci
Design Manager: Kim Winscher
Production Manager: Hollie Kilroy
Photo Researcher: Bryan Stusse
Production: S.E. Anderson

Printed in the China

DEDICATION

To the late extension horticulturist Dr. Sam Cotner, who taught so many Texans how to garden; to retired extension horticulturist and friend Dr. Jerry Parsons, for really *teaching me how to garden; and to my parents, Neil and Jackie Grant, for giving me my first garden plot.*

ACKNOWLEDGMENTS

Greg would like to thank . . .

Bill and Mary Louise Jobe
Bole's Feed
Center Farmer's Market
Cynthia Mueller
Dawn Stover
Greg Smith and family
King's Nursery
Nacogdoches Farmer's Market
SFA Gardens
Stephen F. Austin State University

CONTENTS

WELCOME TO GARDENING IN TEXAS

I'll be honest. Growing fruits and vegetables in Texas isn't easy. It's either too hot, too cold, too wet, or too dry. We alternate from arctic blasts to Mexican heat waves. As I write this, we are in one of the worst droughts in history and just had our hottest month *ever*. Yet you look at the historical data and see that the greatest one-day rainfall in U.S. history was in Alvin, Texas, where it rained 43 inches in 24 hours.

To make matters worse, Texas covers a diverse range of territories, almost like completely different states fused together. We range from a cold winter climate in the north to an almost tropical one in the south. We stretch from a rainfall of 6 inches per year in El Paso to a humid 60 inches in Beaumont. And we go from very alkaline limestone soils in the Texas Hill Country to extremely acid soils in East Texas.

Fruits and vegetables are plagued by all sorts of insects and diseases, plus hungry critters such as crows, squirrels, opossums, raccoons, and deer. When we finally get the soil, water, and temperature conditions right, something else comes along and eats the produce for us. *Why* on earth do I garden here? *Why* would anybody garden here? And why, pray tell, would I try to convince somebody new to attempt such a risky venture?

Because it's magic, that's why. Thomas Jefferson once said, "No occupation is so delightful to me as the culture of the earth, and no culture comparable to that of the garden." Gardening is therapy, both mental and physical. It feeds the mind, body, and soul. And we get to eat the fruits of our labor, even if they don't look like the gargantuan wax-covered commercial versions. There's no substitute for the fresh homegrown taste we harvest from our gardens. Hard, bland, green-picked produce is on the shelf because it ships well, not because it tastes good. And what season goes by without some new disease outbreak or contamination scare linked to mass-produced produce? We have control over that when we grow vegetables in our home gardens.

It's hard to teach about growing produce to such a geographic range of gardeners. But I'll give it my best shot. I learned to garden from my grandfather, Rebel Eloy Emanis, and many others who cared enough to teach me. I'm forever in their debt.

Gardening in Texas isn't really that tough once you learn to play by the rules. It's all about knowing what to grow and when to grow it.

U.S.D.A. Cold Hardiness Zone Map

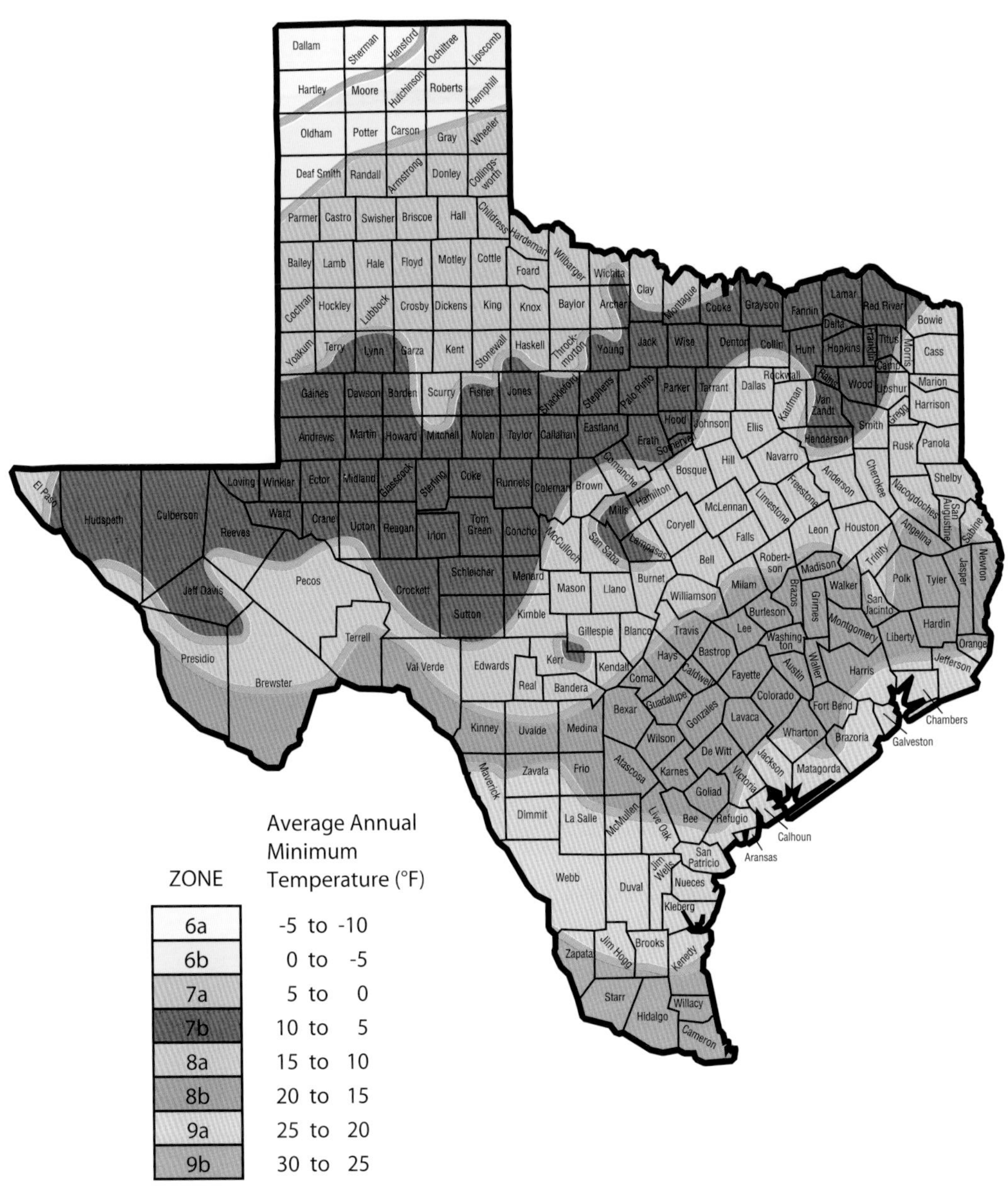

Cold-hardiness zone designations were developed by the United States Department of Agriculture (USDA) to indicate the minimum average temperature for that region. A zone assigned to a plant indicates the lowest temperature at which the plant can normally be expected to survive. Texas has zones ranging from 6a (the coldest) to 9b. Though a plant may grow in zones outside its recommended zone range, the zone ratings are a good indication of which plants to consider for your landscape. Check the map to see which zone your Texas garden is in.

THE GARDEN

HOW TO GET STARTED

My first suggestion for you to get started producing edible crops is to go visit somebody in your area who is doing it. As a matter of fact, visit as many as you can. I've always loved learning from older gardeners who have lived a life producing fruits and vegetables. They've tried it all and can save you lots of trouble. I'm very thankful my grandfather showed me how to run a tiller, how to plow a straight line, how to open a furrow, how to use a hoe, how to pick corn, and numerous other gardening skills. If there's a botanical garden in your area or a Master Gardener group, check to see if they have a demonstration vegetable garden or an orchard that's open to the public. Also ask if they have continuing education classes that cover growing your own edibles. The whole concept is very popular these days, and generally a number of classes and seminars are available.

Be very careful from whom and where you get your advice. Gardening books are wonderful resources, but you

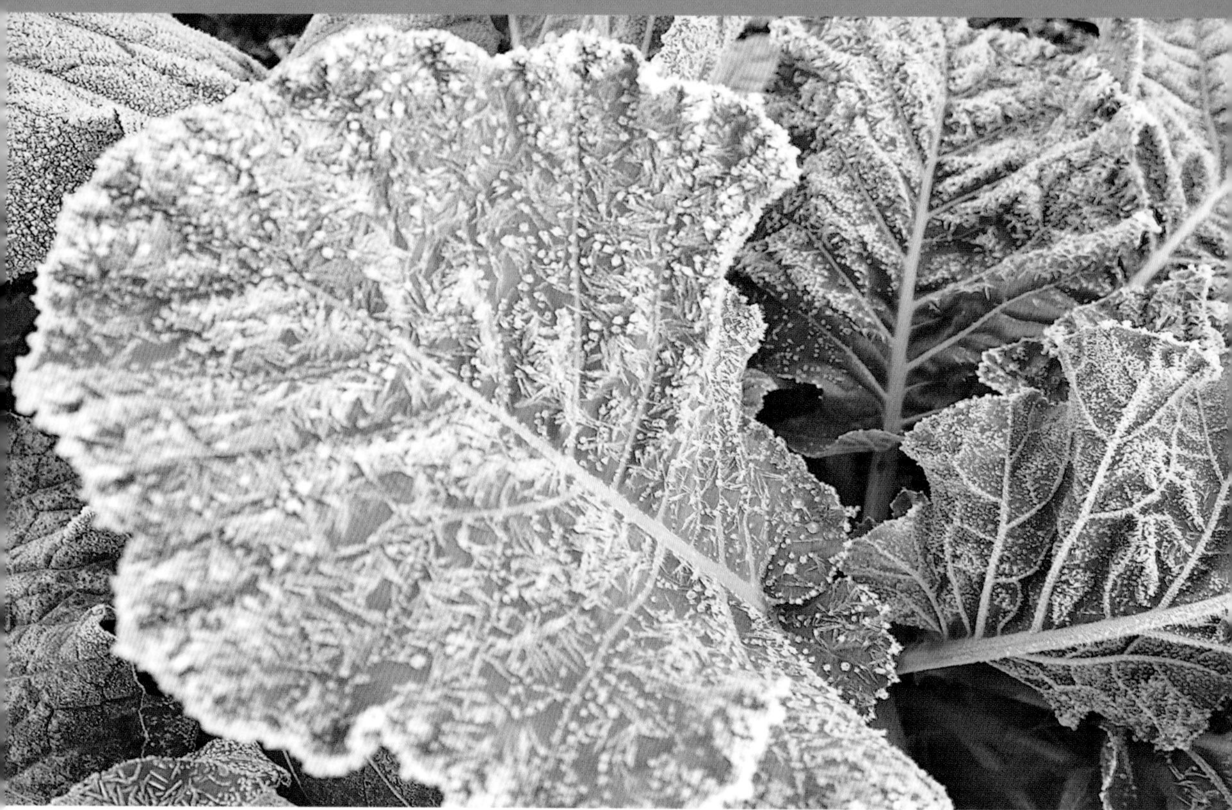

must pay very close attention for what region they are written. Many of them are written for the North, an entirely different gardening climate suited for different vegetables and different planting times than in Texas. I recently borrowed an attractive vegetable gardening book from a friend only to find out it was written in *England* of all places. Don't get me wrong. England is a fabulous country with fabulous gardens and gardeners, but it's pretty much the opposite of Texas when it comes to growing vegetables.

My general rule is, if it grows in Europe and the North, it will suffer or die in the South. And if it thrives in the South, it probably won't grow in Europe or the North. You have to realize that we have no winters equivalent to theirs. This lack of cold eliminates production of certain crops such as cherries here. Our winter is the equivalent of their springtime, so crops they grow in the spring, such as cabbage and broccoli, we grow in the wintertime. Our spring is the equivalent of a Northern or European summer, so their summer crops, such as beans and tomatoes, are our spring crops. And of course they have no equivalent to our summer, so we have to grow an entirely different set of heat-tolerant plants. The reason they don't like okra, sweet potatoes, and Southern peas is because they can't grow them, and if you can't grow them, you can't taste how delicious they are.

Many beginning Texas gardeners make huge mistakes by trying to grow all the things they'd like to eat without finding out whether they will even grow here. Some plants are virtually impossible to produce here, such as rhubarb, raspberries, and apricots. Don't waste money and time on plants that are doomed to failure.

Time of planting is super critical. There are basically three kinds of vegetable crops you can grow: winter (cool-season) plants, spring and fall (mild-season) plants, and heat-loving (hot-season) plants. Spring and fall are pretty much the same in Texas. The temperatures are the same and the day lengths are the same. This means you can basically grow all the same crops in the fall that you do in the spring; you just plant them in reverse order.

For each growing season, sit down with a paper and pencil and plot out what you intend to grow. We can grow crops year-round here and certainly should. Make a winter list, a spring list, a summer list, and a fall list. When one crop is finished, pull it up and put in the next season's plants. Many novice gardeners think spring is the only vegetable-producing time we have—not so. And for heaven's sake if you only grow a garden during the spring, don't let it grow up in weeds when you stop gardening in the summer. This just ensures that you will have weeds forever. It's better to keep it covered with mulch or at least weed free when not in

production. If you don't garden during the summer, plant a cover crop of southern peas or sweet potatoes that can take the heat. The same goes for the winter. At least cover the ground with cereal rye, mustard, or turnips instead of letting it grow up in weeds or have your precious soil wash away in a flood instead.

Be very careful reading seed catalogs or looking at packets on a seed racket. I can assure you the seed companies have never printed a catalog or a seed pack with an ugly picture that says, "This won't grow in Texas." Unfortunately, not all crops and all varieties will grow here. Also be very mindful of the season. Just because you see strawberry plants or tomato plants for sale doesn't mean it's time to plant them. There are many strawberry plants on the shelves in the spring, when it's a season too late to plant them here. There are many tomato transplants on the shelves in May, June, September, and October, when it's too late to plant and produce anything from them here. Get a good Texas gardening calendar each year that shows the proper planting times and be faithful to them. Our land grant university horticulturists spent many years figuring out what would grow here and when to plant it. Don't waste that valuable information.

And please, please, *please* learn to identify a sunny location. Do not confuse *direct sun* (when a beam of light shines directly on you) with *full sun* (a full day's worth of direct sun from the time it rises in the morning until it sets in the evening). Almost all fruits, vegetables, and herbs need full sun, or at the least eight direct hours of it. As my mentor, Dr. Jerry Parsons, always said, "If you can't sunbathe there, you can't grow a vegetable garden, there." Many folks in Texas like to work in the shade, but if you are working in the shade in a vegetable garden you've made a big mistake and your production will suffer immensely. Many beginning gardeners use shade for cooler temperatures as well. This won't work either. For instance, tomatoes need mild temperatures and full sun to set fruit. If you plant them in the shade in July so they will be cooler, they still aren't going to produce because they need full sun to grow.

STARTING AT THE BEGINNING WITH SEEDS

Seeds are amazing dried little parcels that basically contain miniature plants carrying big sack lunches, packaged in protective wrappers. They have everything they need to grow, including genetic instructions for how big to get, what color to be, and how much to produce. They even remember who their parents were! If you are going to be a gardener, you need to know how to grow plants from seed, or at least, the easier ones. Many of the plants grown in a vegetable garden are sown directly into the garden from seed. Others that are more difficult to germinate (sprout) or have slow-growing seedlings are most often grown in a

greenhouse and stepped up into small pots, generally by professional nursery workers. These are sold as transplants, which make it easier and faster for you to produce a crop without all the babysitting.

Whether you buy transplants of such vegetables as tomatoes, peppers, and eggplant, or grow them yourself, always remember that the transplants should *never* stop growing. If they are ever stunted due to lack of fertility, drought, or cold temperatures, their production will be eliminated or severely reduced for the life of the plant. It's better to throw away stunted transplants—no matter how cheap they are or how many you have—than to plant them.

Seed can be obtained from bulk bins at many feed stores, in packages from garden center racks, or from mail-order seed companies. Feed stores generally have tried-and-true varieties that most people in the area have been growing for

years. Seed packs in racks have more of a national selection, so you'll have to be careful what you pick up there, as many won't be adapted to Texas. The price is generally much higher for the seed packets as well. Always make sure the seed packet is fresh and stamped with the current year. Finally, mail-order sources are great for new, improved, and unusual varieties that you can't purchase locally. Just remember to order far in advance so you will have your seed early enough to plant on time. Most seed catalogs (as well as fruit and nut catalogs) are sent out during the winter, which gives you plenty of time to study and dream of things to come in your spring garden. Perusing a plethora of seed catalogs has been a favorite pastime of mine since childhood. They are so full of hope and promise. Just remember they are equally full of heartache and pain. It's best to seek advice from a local gardening expert before you order.

Seed should always be stored in cool, dry conditions. Ziploc bags and glass jars are always handy, as they keep the seeds dry and you can see through them to see how much you have. It's helpful if you fully label each jar or bag of stored seed too. Seed can either be kept in the refrigerator or the freezer. Do not store seeds outside in a shed or a barn, as they won't last very long. Properly stored with cool (or cold), dry conditions, seed can last years and sometimes even decades. Just remember, however, the older the seeds, the fewer will sprout.

Seeds are basically dehydrated, which means they have to absorb moisture before they can grow. Once they absorb moisture, there's no turning back. They either grow or die. With adequate moisture in the soil, they will sprout in days or weeks, depending on the species and the temperature. A general rule of thumb is to plant them the depth of their thickness. In other words, if a seed is 1-inch tall lying down, plant it 1 inch below the soil level. If it's ¼ of an inch tall, plant it ¼ of an inch into the soil. Bigger seeds are planted deeper. Smaller seeds are planted shallow. Oftentimes small seeds are scattered on top of the soil and gently raked in. This ensures that they don't get planted too deeply. If seeds are planted too deep, they are essentially entombed and can't germinate. Tiny, dustlike seed is actually sprinkled on top of the ground without even raking it in. Occasionally, certain seed requires light to germinate and can't be buried at all.

Because seeds have to absorb moisture to awaken and germinate, seed that has historically been hard to sprout is soaked in water overnight or even for several days to speed up the process. When direct planting any kind of seed into the garden, it's important to have adequate soil moisture. If the soil is dry, the seed will just sit there until it rains or you irrigate it. Some gardeners place pieces of wood, burlap sacks, or newspaper over their newly planted seed to conserve moisture while they germinate. If you try this, it's very important to check on its progress daily and remove the covering promptly as the seed sprouts. Once the seeds sprout, they have to have light and room to grow. Clay soils tend to crust over, which prevents tender seedlings from sprouting, so you might want to consider covering them with compost or potting soil instead. I grew up gardening in the sandy soils of northeast Texas. When I took my first vegetable production class at Texas A&M, none of my seeds

germinated in the black clay soil there until I figured out how to cover it with compost instead of clay. We were getting a *grade*, so I had to learn fast!

Many self-sufficient gardeners like to save their own seed instead of purchasing it each year. This works best with heirloom varieties, which come back "true to type." Saved seed from modern hybrids can produce a wide range of offspring not identical to what you originally planted. I love saving my own seed, especially varieties that are hard to find in the trade or that came from a special friend or ancestor. I still grow the same strain of 'Black Crowder' Southern peas that my grandfather did and proudly collect and save the seed each year.

In order to collect seed for next year's crop, the fruit (or vegetable) must be fully mature. Mature fruit is often inedible and slows or stops all production of a plant. I usually designate extra seed-harvesting plants that I've planted at the end of a row, which I don't pick until they are mature and dried. The seed in the fruit that you eat is often tender and not developed. Seed for germinating must be hard and fully mature. Tomatoes with ripe seed will be mushy and almost rotted; cucumbers and squash will be as hard as wood; beans and peas are brown, dried, and shattering; and okra is long, hard, and inedible. Once the mature hard seed is extracted from a fruit, let it completely dry before packaging it, labeling it, and storing it in a cool (or cold) dry place until next year.

CREATING THE PERFECT SOIL

If you are going to garden, you are going to have to learn to get down and dirty. There's no other way. I've never thought of soil as dirty. The terms that come to mind are wholesome, earthy, and natural. Plants need soil for their roots to grow in. The roots provide anchorage and absorb water and nutrients from the soil. There are different types of soil with different properties. It's best if you learn to identify them so you'll know what your strengths and weaknesses are. Only add amendments to your soil when you know *why* you are adding them. You may not need to add anything.

Sand Silt Loam Clay Soil

A few definitions are in order. All soils are made up of four types of substances in assorted proportions: minerals, organics, air, and water. All are essential to plant growth. Mineral soils are divided into three types, which are based on their particle size: sand, silt, and clay. Sand is comprised of large particles, which makes it drain extremely well, generally too well. Sandy soils dry out quickly and do not retain nutrients for very long, as they leach out with the water as it's draining. They are easy to work, however. Sandy soils are often described as loose or light. Clay is comprised of very small, flat, slippery particles that don't drain very well but do hold fast to nutrients and water. They are very difficult to work and cultivate. Clay soils are often described as tight and heavy. Clay soils tend to stick to your shoes and tiller and dry into large clods or "bricks." Silt is comprised of medium-sized particles with intermediate characteristics between sand and clay. Loam soils have equal portions of sand, silt, and clay, and they are ideal for gardening as they provide the benefits of each. Most vegetable gardeners prefer a sandy loam soil. These ideal soils are often referred to as friable, crumbly, and loamy—they all mean the same texture.

Of course, describing the ideal soil and owning the ideal soil are completely different things. The best way to improve your soil is with the addition of organic matter. Organic matter improves the moisture- and nutrient-holding capacities of sandy soils, and it improves the drainage, aeration, and workability of clay soils. Without air, roots can't take up nutrients and plants will be stunted or even die from root rot. Organic matter can come from home compost piles made from decayed leaves, grass clippings, and table scraps, or it can be purchased as compost, mushroom compost, composted cotton seed hulls, or composted black pine bark. Never let any organic matter go to waste. Noncomposted organic matter, such

Creating the Perfect Soil

as leaves, hay, rice hulls, pine bark, and pine straw, can be placed on top of the ground where it will prevent weeds, retain moisture, and keep the ground cooler in the summer and warmer in the winter. As it decomposes, it improves your soil.

The acidity of different soils is measured by its pH. The pH scale runs from 1 to 14 with most soils falling between 5 and 8. Low pH soils (less than 7.0) are acidic while high pH soils (greater than 7.0) are alkaline. A neutral soil has a pH of 7.0. Acid soils "tie up" (prevent the absorption of) a number of major nutrients and waste your fertilizer. If your soil is very acidic, add lime or wood ashes to raise the pH. Alkaline soils don't allow your plants to take up iron and other micronutrients. This often results in plants with yellow new leaves or iron chlorosis. If your soil is too alkaline, you will need to add sulfur or aluminum sulfate. It's best to strive for a neutral or slightly acidic soil for the best gardening results.

Most vegetables are heavy feeders. We expect a lot of production from them. This means our soils have to be fertile. It's best to have a soil test done, which will tell you the pH of your soil along with levels of major and minor nutrients. Plants use more nitrogen (N), phosphorus (P), and potassium (K) than any other nutrients. These are termed macronutrients. By law, all containers of fertilizer list the percentages of these three macronutrients within that specific fertilizer.

So when you see a bag of 15-5-10 fertilizer, this means it contains 15 percent nitrogen (N), 5 percent phosphorus (P), and 10 percent potassium (K). The bag will also list all other macro and minor nutrients contained within that specific

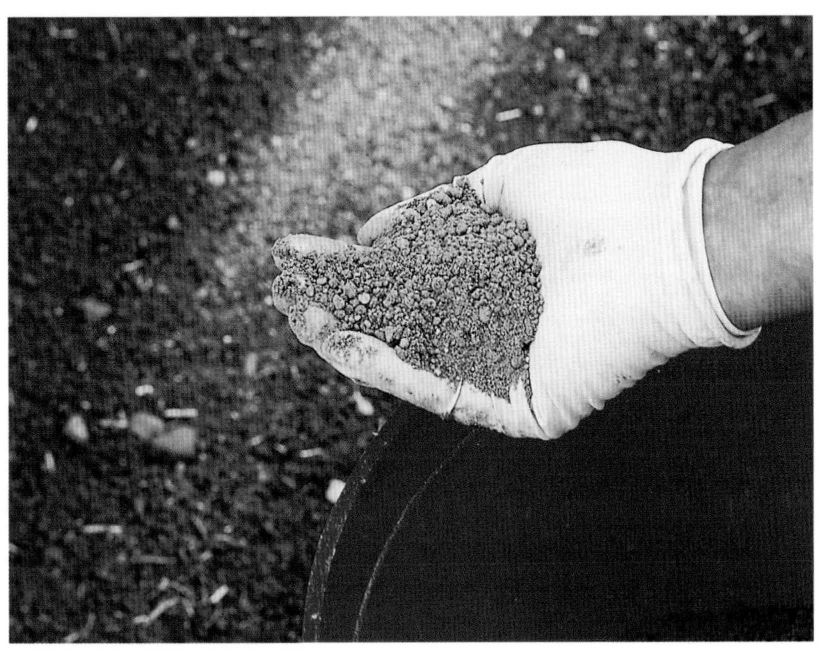

fertilizer. Man-made fertilizers are manufactured from nonliving products and byproducts and are generally referred to as inorganic fertilizers. They are higher in nutrients than organic fertilizers. Organic fertilizers are made from products or byproducts of living organisms and are lower in nutrients. This means you have to use greater quantities of organic fertilizers to obtain the same amount of nutrients. It's not unusual to see organic fertilizers with an analysis such as 1-1-1 or 5-2-1. Organic fertilizers often used in home vegetable production include chicken litter, cow manure, horse manure, rabbit manure, cottonseed meal, and fish emulsion. I have access to chicken litter and cow manure and certainly make use of every drop of it.

A preplant application of fertilizer is generally applied so that the vegetables will be healthy, well fed, and actively

Water-Soluble Fertilizer

growing from the time they germinate or are transplanted. It's very important that vegetables never be stressed from starvation, as production will be either eliminated or severely reduced. On the other hand, overfertilization can lead to plant death or excessive growth of foliage, which may result in reduced fruit production or plants that break apart or collapse.

Pay close attention to the type of soil you have and the type vegetables, herbs, or fruits that you want to grow. Certain types of plants require certain types of soils. Root crops, such as carrots and potatoes, do best in loose, well-drained sandy soils. If you don't have such soil, you will need to create it. If amending your existing soil isn't practical, you might want to build raised beds where you bring in a "ready to go" soil mix, such as mushroom compost. Always remember that adding decomposed organic matter or compost can improve your existing soil. If you add organic matter that hasn't decomposed or broken down (not composted), it will rob nitrogen from the soil while it does, resulting in stunted yellow plants. Many rookie organic gardeners fall prey to hungry plants by adding noncomposted organic matter to their soils without adding additional nitrogen to help it decompose and for the hungry plants to feed on. Since vegetables are heavy feeders, most of them will require adding fertilizer or sidedressing regularly while they are growing and producing. A good rule of thumb is to add small amounts of fertilizer often as opposed to large amounts of fertilizer infrequently.

COMPOSTING

Composting is the biological breakdown of organic matter by a managed process. The resulting compost is a decomposed humus-like organic matter, which generally improves the structure of all soils and releases small amounts of beneficial nutrients. Every home gardener should compost. It should be a law! It's an easy way to produce your own potting soil and fertilizer at home without wasting valuable space at the local landfill. There are entire publications and websites devoted to composting that can frankly leave a beginning gardener quite bewildered and less than enthusiastic. If you can't handle it, don't read it! The best advice about composting comes from my good friend and fellow garden writer Felder Rushing. His now famous two-part instructions are: "Stop throwing that stuff away" and, "Pile it up somewhere." He's right. All organic matter breaks down, a process that's even faster in our hot and often humid state.

To speed things up a bit, here are the basics. There are two general components that you will be saving and adding to your compost pile: dry brown matter, which is high in carbon, and animal waste or green matter, which is high in

nitrogen. Instead of throwing away or hauling off grass clippings, leaves, weeds, small prunings, dead plants, used potting soil, kitchen scraps, or animal manures (from plant-eating animals), all of these belong in your compost pile. The main organic things you want to avoid are meat scraps, dairy products, oils, noxious weeds, diseased plants, and dog and cat waste.

Materials to be composted are ideally piled in alternating layers, with nitrogen-rich materials sandwiched in 1-inch layers between 6 to 8 inches of dried, brown, carbon-rich materials. To heat up and break down faster, the pile must be slightly moist and well aerated. Many commercial composting bins are available, or you can make your own out of anything from mesh fence wire to cinder blocks or pallets. Remember, the bigger the better. If you don't have access to any of those bin materials, just pile the compost out of the way somewhere and wait. Once the materials break down, you have your own, free, magic organic matter that can be used as mulch, soil amendment, or potting soil.

COMPOST TROUBLESHOOTING

Symptoms	Problems	Solutions
The compost has a bad odor.	Not enough air. Pile is too wet.	Turn/mix it. Add coarse dry materials such as straw, corn stalks, or leaves.
The center of the pile is dry.	Not enough water. Too much dry, woody, coarse material.	Turn and moisten materials. Add fresh green waste. Chop or shred coarse materials into smaller particles.
The compost is damp and warm in the middle but nowhere else.	Pile is too small.	Collect more materials and mix the old ingredients into a new pile.
The pile is damp and sweet-smelling but still will not heat up.	Lack of nitrogen.	Mix in a nitrogen source like fresh grass clippings, fresh manure, or a high-nitrogen fertilizer.

CONTAINER GARDENING

Container gardening sounds very appealing, and it is for those who have no *terra firma* in which to garden. Just be warned that gardening in containers in Texas is harder than gardening in the ground. There are a number of issues that you will be forced to deal with.

The number one limiting factor with container gardening in Texas is water. Due to gravity from the raised pots and the limited amount of soil contained in them, containers in Texas often have to be watered as much as twice a day to survive and produce. If a single watering is missed on a hot, dry day, the fruit or vegetable plants will be stressed or killed, or, at the least, their production will be aborted.

There are two main ways to avoid frequent drought stress when container gardening. The first is using the largest pot

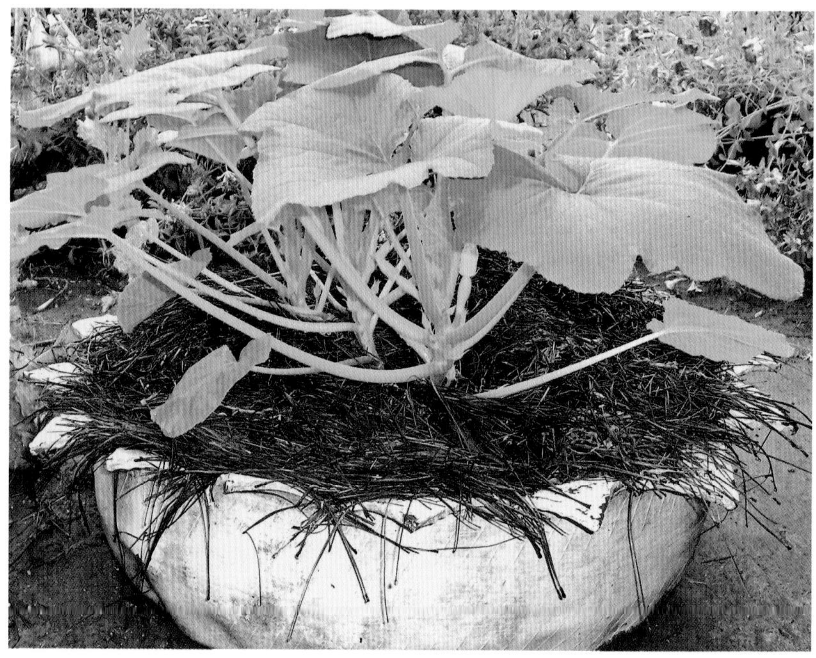

size you can find or afford. The larger the container you use, the more soil mix it will hold and the slower it will dry out. Larger containers allow plants to have larger root systems, which are more adept at avoiding drought stress. I personally consider whiskey barrel–sized containers the minimum size for home fruit and vegetable production. I've also had good success with galvanized farm-watering troughs and homemade crown tire planters. My uncle Noel has long used large plastic nursery pots that were previously used for growing trees. Any large container will work as long as there are drainage holes in the bottom.

When watering, it's extremely important to soak the entire soil area from top to bottom. Oftentimes, especially when the soil is dry in pots, water will just run off the top and down the inside of the container without soaking the root zone. Use low-pressure drip irrigation to soak the entire root zone as it slowly waters the plants with little runoff.

The soil mix, media, or potting soil you use in containers will also spell the difference between success and failure. There are two choices that you want to avoid. Topsoil dug from the ground is extremely heavy, and though it may drain

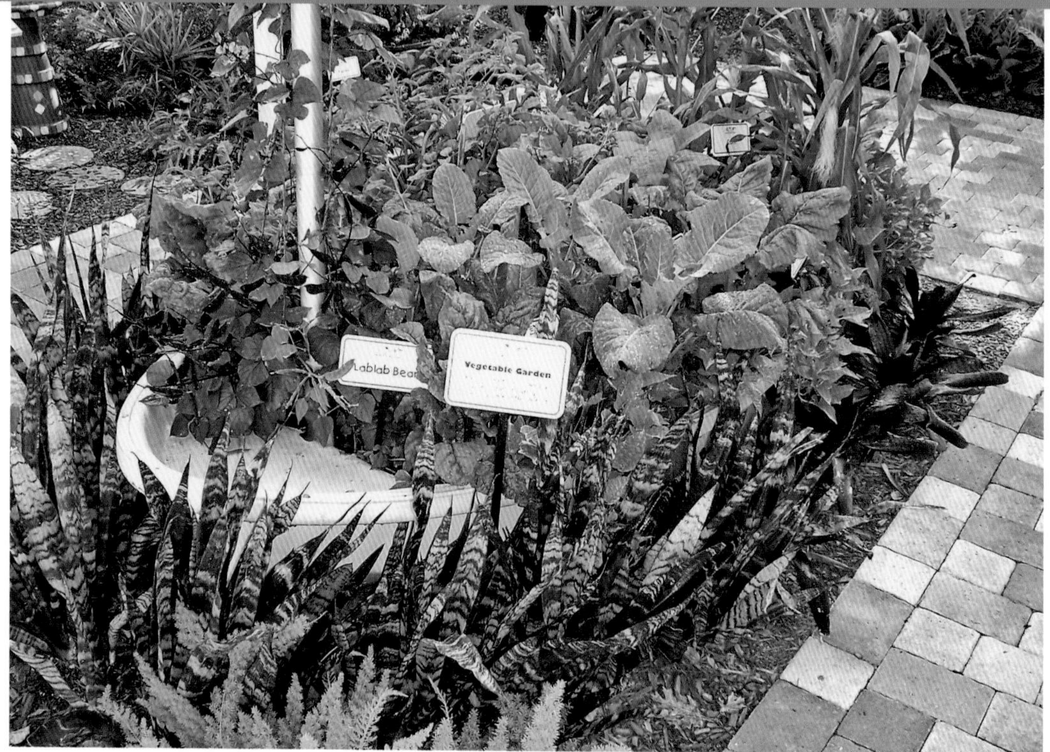

well in the ground, it will not drain well in a container. Composted black pine bark, which the nursery industry uses to grow containerized shrubs and trees, is not a good choice either, as it drains too well and doesn't retain nutrients.

Though you can experiment with mixtures of compost, washed sand, and topsoil, for most beginners the best option is a professional-grade, peat-based potting soil. Just remember that there are three grades of potting soil. Inexpensive potting soils are made from composted pine bark and can be tricky. Medium-priced potting soils are made from muck peat and do a fair job of producing plants. Professional-grade potting soils are made from sphagnum peat moss and do the best job of producing vegetables in containers. They cost more but are worth it, especially for a beginner. These mixtures, which are used by most greenhouse growers in the country, have good water- and nutrient-holding capacities, which makes all the difference in the world in container gardening.

As a gardener, you need to know that sand, pine bark, and perlite are known for increasing drainage (adding aeration) but not for retaining nutrients. Finished compost, vermiculite, and sphagnum peat moss are known for retaining both water and nutrients. Plants that produce edible crops are very heavy feeders and need constant high fertility (they needs lots of fertilizer). Container plants lose many of their nutrients through leaching, where the water-soluble nutrients run out of the bottom of the pot. Using a slow-release fertilizer, such as Osmocote, in a container will help provide constant nutrition without leaching. Slow-release fertilizers may not provide all the nutrition your container plants need and may have to be supplemented with water-soluble fertilizers (such as Miracle Gro and others) as needed.

WATERING IN THE GARDEN

Watering is not an option in Texas—it is a must. Generally we have moisture in the winter, spring, and fall with long extended droughts during the summer. Most plants require the equivalent of 1 to 2 inches of rainfall per week. If the plants don't receive it in the form of rain, then they need it through supplemental irrigation.

You have four options for applying water to your fruits and vegetables: by hand, with overhead sprinklers, with furrow or flood irrigation, with low-volume drip irrigation. Of course, hand watering is only practical for a limited number of plants, including container plants. Always remember that you will have to water larger containers less frequently than smaller containers. I personally would never plant in any container smaller than whiskey-barrel sized. With smaller containers all you have to do is miss a single day's watering during a hot, dry period to stunt or kill your plants. Also be sure to use a soil mix that has the capacity to retain water; otherwise you will be watering them twice a day during our typical summers. Commercial-grade potting soils do the best job, but a good potting soil is certainly possible to make at home. Just remember that well-drained garden soil from the ground is rarely well draining in a container and is generally extremely heavy.

Overhead sprinklers are quite common and readily available. However, they waste large amounts of water due to evaporation, and they promote diseases by wetting the leaves on plants. If you are forced to use overhead irrigation, early morning is best, so that the foliage and fruit can dry off as soon as the sun comes out. Fruit and foliage that is wet all night can lead to disease problems.

Furrow and flood irrigation are old-fashioned methods of watering where the irrigation water is run down furrows,

basins, or channels next to the plants. You must have a gentle slope and, of course, prepared furrows for this to work. I use furrow irrigation for the large row-crop vegetable garden at my farm. It puts the water where the plants need it and not on the foliage. It's the same system my grandfather taught me to use. If your rows have too much slope, you won't get enough absorption on the upper parts of the rows—a gentle slope is the key. The other option is a level furrow, with high banks or sides that hold the water in.

Drip irrigation is very popular these days, as it doesn't require much pressure and doesn't waste water or promote foliage and fruit diseases. Emitters are placed directly next to the desirable plants so only those plants—not the weeds and bare surrounding ground—receive the irrigation water. I've been working hard over the last decade to increase my use of more drip irrigation. There are systems with preplaced holes in the lines or those where you insert the emitters where you want them. I've used both, depending how close together my plants are. I program timers attached to my faucets so they run as long as I want them to, then they turn off on their own, according to the schedule I've set.

Rainfall and runoff capture is also another popular concept these days. Like all my ancestors, I have a cistern at the back of my house, which catches the rainfall that runs off from my roof. It's silly and wasteful to allow rainfall to run straight into the gutter and down the storm drains instead of replenishing our gardens, pastures, prairies, forests, and aquifers.

Remember that too much water can be as devastating, if not more so, than too little. It's okay for plants to wilt just a bit from drought, but if they are kept too wet, their roots rot and it's much harder (if not impossible) to revive the plants. Also remember that plants take up water through their roots, not their leaves. Wetting the foliage on plants leads to a multitude of diseases. If you must wet the foliage on your plants, do it in the morning so that they will be dry by nightfall.

PEST CONTROL

Unfortunately, everything likes to eat fruits and vegetables. Please don't get discouraged when you find that you have rotted fruit or plants chewed to the ground. You are not alone. Everybody faces the same issues, including professional farmers and horticulturists. I've always said that all gardeners kill the same number of plants. The only difference is good gardeners pull them up and move on to the next crop, while brown thumbs just give up and stare at them.

Plant diseases are sure to be an issue. Unfortunately, diseases can't be cured, only prevented. It helps to learn how to recognize what the problem is. Plant diseases are most commonly caused by viruses, bacteria, and fungi. Viruses cause plants to be stunted and mottled or variegated, with assorted, often random, yellow and green patterns on their foliage, as viruses interfere with chlorophyll production.

Viruses are spread to plants by piercing, sucking insects, such as aphids, white flies, and leaf hoppers. There is no cure for plants infected by a virus. Affected plants should be pulled up and destroyed to keep them from infecting your other plants. The same virus doesn't affect all vegetable plants, only those that are the same species or related and in the same family. Tomatoes, peppers, and squash are the vegetables most likely to be infected by a virus. Though they're still edible, virus-infected squash are often spotted with green and yellow. When you control piercing-sucking insects you help prevent virus infection.

Bacterial diseases generally cause spotted foliage or rotted fruit. Excess water on a plant often causes these problems to develop. It's important to remember that plants drink water through their roots, not their foliage, so drip irrigation will help prevent foliage diseases. Bacterial leaf spots are small spots on the leaves surrounded by dark, water-soaked halos, where the bacteria are actually dissolving the leaf. Bacterial rots cause soft, smelly decay in the fruits. Sanitation is the most important defense against bacterial diseases. Always remove infected plants and fruits, and do not put them in the compost pile. Rake up and discard any infected leaves and stems as well.

Fungal diseases can cause leaf spots too. These spots are often surrounded by dry, tan, or brown tissue and concentric circles or rings. Though you can't cure these spots, you can prevent new foliage from being affected by applying an appropriately labeled fungicide, which protects the healthy foliage.

Keeping the foliage dry will help prevent fungal diseases, as the fungal spores can germinate only on wet foliage. Fungal diseases of the root system can also cause rapid wilting and death of an entire plant. It's important to make sure to rotate your crops by planting them in different areas each year. Since specific soil borne diseases only affect certain plants, this helps keep infection down. Planting in raised beds and rows also improves drainage, which helps prevent fungal root rots. As with bacterial diseases, sanitation is the most important defense against fungal diseases. Fungal spores lie dormant in dead plant parts, debris, and soil. Always remove and

destroy all infected plants, fruit, and foliage from your garden to prevent future infection.

Nematodes are microscopic worm-like organisms that infect the root systems of certain kinds of plants. They cause hundreds of swollen knots on the root system that lead to stunted plants. Figs, tomatoes, and okra are the most common victims. They are typically associated with sandy soils. There is no control for nematodes, though planting a cool-season cover crop of Elbon cereal rye, and tilling it under while green, can help control their numbers. Crop rotation is extremely important in avoiding nematode problems.

Birds can be devastating to tomatoes and most fruit crops. Mockingbirds, woodpeckers, and crows are three common culprits. Gardeners have tried many scare tactics through the years, including aluminum pie plates, colored streamers, fake ripe fruit, noisemakers, and, of course, scarecrows. Unfortunately, the birds quickly get used to all of these. The only surefire way of preventing bird damage to your precious crop is by covering an entire plant with bird netting, which can be purchased from your local home-improvement stores, garden centers, or hardware stores.

Other animals that prove quite frustrating to home gardening are deer, armadillos, opossums, raccoons, and

squirrels. My family has always employed terriers (rat and Jack Russell) for varmint control. (And you thought I only kept Rosie and Molly around because they were cute.) They are quite effective. Live traps can be successful for capturing smaller critters. High fencing, deer repellent, and monofilament fishing line strung through the garden work better for Bambi and his kin.

Insects and their relatives will most likely be your main problem in producing edible crops at home. First, it's important to realize that not all insects and critters are harmful to your crops. Learn the good guys and protect them, as they are nature's insecticide. Ladybugs, assassin bugs, praying mantis, lacewings, wasps, spiders, anoles (lizards), and most songbirds are insect eaters and should be preserved and promoted. Second, learn the harmful insects, such as aphids, stinkbugs, white flies, potato bugs, tomato hornworms, cabbage loopers, and corn ear worms, and determine the level of infestation you can stand before you need to treat them. Remember they are food for other creatures and that small, minimally damaging populations can certainly be tolerated. Never forget that organically-produced crops generally have some insect damage while spectacular-looking produce has often received regular applications of insecticide.

Remember that all pollinators are beneficial and can easily be harmed by pesticides. Bees, flies, wasps, butterflies, and hummingbirds all help pollinate our crops and should be cherished and considered when making pesticide applications.

ORGANIC GARDENING

Organic gardening is very trendy these days. It is a noble and worthy cause, and I hope you will give it a try. Basically, it means gardening without man-made chemical fertilizers and pesticides. Handling the plant diseases organically is only a small challenge in my book. Most diseases can be controlled through varietal selection, planting time, and cultural control. Insects are a little trickier, but a number of organic pesticides are on the market and can make the job easier. Of course, there's always the old-fashioned way of picking the pests off by hand and dropping them in a bucket of soapy water.

Fertilizing organically is a tougher chore, however. There are two very important nutritional aspects to organic gardening that you *must* be aware of. First and foremost,

most vegetables and fruits are heavy feeders that require regular fertilization. For plants to be productive, they must take up lots of nutrients. If you expect to be fed well, feed your plants well. Plants that require little supplemental nutrition, like figs, are the exception rather than the rule. Unfortunately, organic fertilizers are low in nitrogen and other nutrients, which means you have to apply them in greater quantities and more often than you would chemical fertilizers. In my opinion, most beginning organic gardens fail due to lack of available nutrients for their plants. I've seen many vegetable gardens, both organic and otherwise, literally starved to death, inhabited by stunted and yellow (nitrogen-deficient) plants.

It's extremely important to realize that added organic matter, such as leaves, straw, rice hulls, and bark, uses up and depletes nitrogen until it is broken down (by being composted). Coarse, nondecomposed organic materials are better used as mulch on top of the ground instead of as soil amendments. Once they break down and decompose, they release nitrogen back into the soil, improve the structure of the soil, and increase the water- and nutrient-holding capacities of the soil.

GARDENING WITH CHILDREN

Gardening as a child literally changed my life. It gave me a lifelong connection with nature, the outdoors, science, hard work, and healthy nutrition. Unfortunately, today most children are disconnected from the outdoor environment. Humans were made to till the soil and harvest their own food. It just doesn't seem natural to me to do otherwise. Children are like dry sponges when they are young, soaking up new ideas, concepts, knowledge, and habits. Why not start them on the road to a physically and mentally healthy life by encouraging them to garden?

Miss Mozelle, my legendary first grade teacher at Mozelle Johnston Elementary School in Longview, Texas, appointed me keeper of the class terrarium in first grade. She was a *real* teacher and knew just what each student needed to learn. My fourth grade teacher, Mrs. Sandra Field, allowed me to read a book about George Washington Carver, which immediately inspired my horticultural career goals. Old Mr. Adams, up the hill and through the woods, let me help him garden and taught me how to grow potatoes. I'll never forget putting pieces of potatoes in the ground and later bringing a sack full of whole potatoes home to my mom . . . pure magic. My grandfather, Eloy Emanis, taught me how to produce all the common vegetable crops, and my grandmother, Marquette Emanis, showed me how to put them up and prepare them. And, of course, my parents, Neil and Jackie Grant, assigned me my

own separate patch of the vegetable garden to do with as I pleased. It didn't take long for them to realize how interested I was. They quickly turned the whole garden over to me, and to this day I produce all the vegetables for the entire family.

An entire school curriculum could be taught from an outdoor gardening environment, including history, biology, chemistry, literature, art, and more. It's all there. Unlike classroom learning, it's hands-on and interactive. It's hard not to be interested and learn when something's growing before your very eyes, thanks to your own input. And, of course, the beauty of the whole setup is you get to eat your homework! There's no reason the dog should have all the fun.

For children's gardens, it's best to start small. If experienced adults will be helping, an open patch with tilled rows will work. However, in most cases a raised bed, as small as 3 × 8 feet, is a good place to start. It can easily be filled with a professional-grade potting soil or a vegetable garden mix from a local landscape supply company or home-improvement store. If drip irrigation is installed along with a generous mulch of straw or dried grass clippings, watering and weeding will be much simplified.

It's important to choose crops that are easy to grow so that children will feel successful. That's why radishes always end up in children's gardens. Unfortunately, most kids won't

eat radishes. So it's better to plant some things they are more likely to eat. Salad gardens—complete with assorted lettuces, cabbage, broccoli, carrots, and so forth—are popular at many schools. The kids all enjoy both making and eating the salads they've produced. It's extremely important to have volunteers helping who will ensure the crops produce, since the kids will be beginners and won't know how. Many school gardens end up full of starving, stunted plants surrounded by weeds. Try to make sure to provide success and a model of what a good garden should look like. And make sure there's a good cook around to show them how they can eat them. Most children will say they don't like tomatoes but don't have any idea that there wouldn't be ketchup, pizza, or spaghetti sauce without them. Heck, most of them don't have a clue that McDonald's french fries started out in the dirt somewhere.

Tell them stories, take them on farm or garden field trips, show them things, let them touch and feel, scratch and sniff. When I was teaching horticulture at Louisiana State University, I taught a weekly first grade gardening class at the local lab school on campus. Those kids loved parading around behind me. We planted stuff, picked stuff, ate stuff, climbed trees, played in the mud, drew pictures, sang songs, and learned all kinds of stuff. Learning should be interesting and fun. We don't have a choice. All folks have to eat vegetables to live a healthy disease-free life. The earlier we learn it, the better off we are.

HARVEST & STORAGE

Knowing when to pick and how to store your produce is an important key in enjoying and eating it. As a general rule, all produce should be harvested early in the morning, when it is crisp and full of water. Nobody likes limp vegetables. It's also critical that you avoid damaging your produce when picking or digging it. Every wound or scar is a point of entry for diseases, not to mention an aesthetic blemish. It's always a good idea to eat the damaged produce immediately and store the good-looking ones. Most tender vegetables require high humidity and low temperatures for optimum storage conditions. It's best to put them in plastic bags and into the refrigerator or crisper as soon as possible after picking to ensure freshness and flavor. A few vegetables, such as Irish potatoes, sweet potatoes, pumpkins, winter squash, and onions, are best stored dry at moderately cool temperatures to prevent them from rotting. And for heaven's sake, remember that most vegetables are more tender and better tasting when picked on the small side instead of back-breaking jumbos. Giant cucumbers and zucchinis aren't edible and should be discarded. The reason shoppers pay premium prices for baby vegetables is their high quality.

Palmetto PRIDE
STAKE
SILV SHOWER TM AZTEC

VEGETABLES & HERBS

Growing your own produce is fulfilling and rewarding. There's nothing so gratifying as growing your own food from seeds or transplants. Not only does it feel better than purchasing produce from the grocery store, but as all home gardeners know, it tastes better as well. It also saves you money and saves fuel costs. And more important, you know exactly where it's been, who has handled it, what fertilizer was used on it, and what pesticides have been sprayed on it. And because you only have to haul it to your kitchen, you are able to let the produce mature until the peak of full-flavored ripeness. Commercial vendors have to pick their crops before they are ripe so they can be shipped and handled. Thanks to home gardening, your taste buds will rejoice.

ARUGULA

Arugula (*Eruca vesicaria sativa*) is a trendy green that appears in many salad mixes these days. I have loved it since the first time my friend and mentor Bill Welch introduced it to me years ago in College Station. To me, its flavor presents a unique taste blend of mustard and peanuts.

When to Plant

Arugula is a cool-weather plant that goes to seed when the weather is hot. Its flavor gets stronger and the leaves get tougher with heat as well. Arugula can tolerate frosts but not hard freezes, so it should be planted in late winter or early spring for an initial crop. A second fall crop can be planted around September in the northern half of Texas and in October in the southern half of Texas. Arugula can either be direct seeded or planted as transplants, which are often available from nurseries and garden centers. After the new seedlings are established, thin them to 4 to 6 inches apart.

Where to Plant

Arugula requires at least eight hours of direct sun each day, but like most greens it can tolerate a bit of filtered light, or as little as five to six hours of direct sun. Just remember that any amount of shade reduces production. Plant arugula in rich, well-drained soil, either in the ground or in containers at least 12 inches in diameter. Small containers dry out quickly in Texas's frequent warm temperatures, leading to plant death or stress.

Ideally, till several inches of organic matter into the soil and apply 2 pounds of a complete garden fertilizer (15-5-10, 13-13-13, and so forth) per 100 square feet of bed or every 35 feet of row. In small plots, use 2 teaspoons per square foot or foot row. The ideal soil pH for growing arugula is 5.5 to 7.0.

How to Plant

Arugula can either be grown in beds or rows several feet apart. If you are direct seeding, scatter the seed on tilled soil that has been raked smooth. *Gently* rake the seed into the soil, making sure that it is no deeper than ¼ of an inch below the surface of the soil. Water gently and carefully, and keep the soil moist until germination (sprouting) occurs. Then reduce the *frequency* of watering so that the plants gradually get tougher and dry out slightly. Transplants should be placed 6 inches apart in holes dug into well-prepared soil that are the same size as the existing rootball. Water well with a water-soluble plant food such as Miracle Gro at half the labeled recommendation.

Care and Maintenance

The keys to growing good arugula are cool temperatures, high fertility, and frequent harvesting. To keep leaves fresh and tender, shear the entire plant with hedge clippers every two to three weeks and side-dress with a high-nitrogen granular fertilizer, such as ammonium sulfate (21-0-0, and so forth), at 2 pounds per 35 feet of row. Slugs as well as foliage-eating insects can be a problem, especially during warm weather. Pick off the buggy leaves and treat the plants with an insecticide labeled for greens (and the bug), if necessary.

Harvest

Arugula is usually ready to harvest in thirty to forty days from seed. Transplants can be ready to harvest in several weeks. Pick or snip young foliage that is free of insect damage, wash it, and serve or refrigerate it immediately. Harvest early in the morning for the freshest leaves. Avoid picking during hot weather, as the flavor will be strong and hot.

Additional Information

I like the flavor of arugula as is. However *some* feel it's too strong and are happier mixing it with lettuce and other salad greens. It's also called roquette or rocket. Recommended varieties include 'Apollo', 'Wild Sylvetta', and 'Roquette'. Arugula is native to the Mediterranean.

ASPARAGUS

There are generally two types of people, those who love fresh-picked asparagus (*Asparagus officinalis*) and those who have never tried it. Adding to that divide is the misconception that asparagus is hard to grow. This couldn't be further from the truth. As a matter of fact, my start of this tasty delicacy came from an old abandoned home place, growing in the middle of a pasture. The most important thing to remember is that the delicious shoots you harvest each spring are courtesy of energy stored in the root system from last year's abundant foliage.

When to Plant

Asparagus is planted from dormant roots or crowns, which can generally be purchased during the winter and early spring. Crowns should look healthy and shouldn't be dried out. It is best to plant them immediately after purchasing. However, they can be kept in a plastic bag in the refrigerator for up to a week. Asparagus crowns should be spaced at least 18 inches apart.

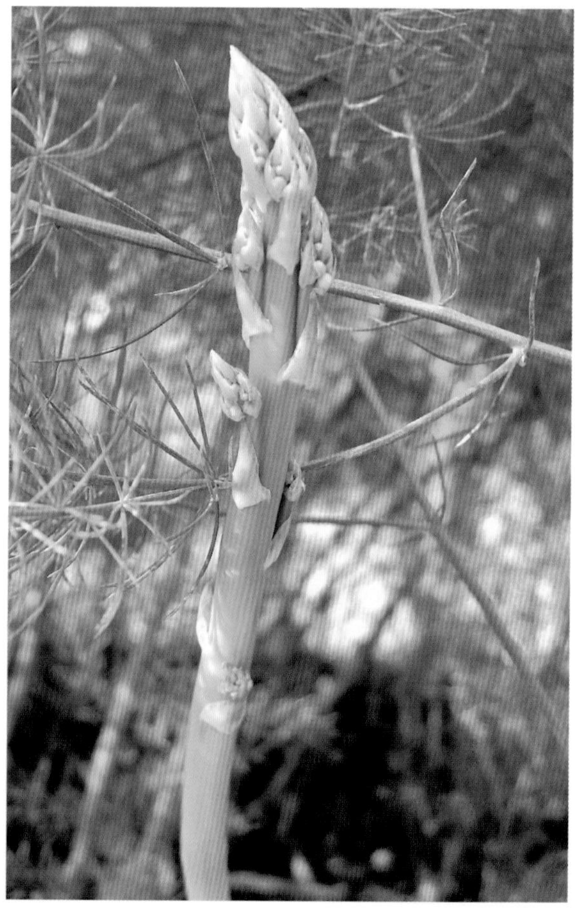

Where to Plant

Asparagus produces best in a well-drained soil amended with organic matter in a location that receives direct sun at least eight hours a day. Many successful gardeners plant their asparagus in beds 3 to 4 feet wide that are amended with 3 to 4 inches of organic matter and a complete lawn or garden fertilizer (15-5-10, 13-13-13, and so forth) at 2 pounds per 100 square feet of bed area. Spade or till to a generous depth of 10 to 12 inches. The ideal soil pH for asparagus is 6.0 to 6.7

How to Plant

The crowns should be planted 18 inches apart in rows or beds that are at least 4 feet apart. In loose, sandy soils, plant them 10 inches deep. In heavier clay soils, plant them 6 to 8 inches deep. Cover them with well-prepared soil and water them immediately. A 2- to 4-inch covering of mulch, such as pine straw, clean hay, or grass clippings, will help prevent weeds and keep the root system warmer in the winter and cooler in the summer.

Care and Maintenance

Asparagus has very few insect or disease problems. It's all about growing the biggest plants you can during the growing season so that you can harvest the succulent spears for three to four weeks the following spring. Fertilize the plants with a complete lawn or garden fertilizer (15-5-10, 13-13-13, and so forth) each spring and provide them with the equivalent of an inch of water per week during the growing season. Keep the bed weed free to prevent competition. Harvest no shoots or spears during the first two years. Each year the 3- to 5-foot foliage will go dormant during the wintertime and should be cut and discarded. During the third growing season, all tender green asparagus shoots may be harvested for up to a month during the early spring if they are plentiful. It's imperative that all shoots are harvested during this period to encourage the plant to continue to produce new shoots. Fertilize the plants as soon as you finish harvesting with a complete lawn or garden fertilizer, and mulch the plant generously to prevent weeds during the summer.

Harvest

Do not harvest at all the first two growing seasons. Starting in the third year, harvest the young tender spears when they are about 6 inches long, before they have started making foliage and will easily snap off in your hand. The sooner you cook them, the better they taste.

Additional Information

Asparagus has been cultivated almost since the beginning of history, as the elite of the Egyptian, Greek, and Roman societies enjoyed it as a treasured culinary delicacy. Recommended asparagus varieties for Texas include 'UC 157', 'Jersey Knight', 'Jersey Giant', and 'Jersey Gem'. Asparagus is native to the Mediterranean and Asia Minor.

BASIL

This wonderful aromatic herb is included in many dishes these days and is a must for tomato sauces and Italian dishes. Of course pesto, a ground combination of fresh basil (*Ocimum basilicum*), garlic, nuts, olive oil and Parmesan cheese goes well with just about anything. A little bit of basil goes a long way, so often a single plant provides enough for a small family. There are many different flavored basils, but my favorite is the large-leafed sweet basil.

When to Plant

Although it is fairly easy to grow from seed, basil is generally planted from transplants after all danger of frost in the spring. Basil thrives with mild and moderately warm temperatures but cannot tolerate a frost or freeze. If summer heat and drought kill your initial planting, another crop can be planted in early autumn. Although a single plant is generally enough for a small family, an 18-inch spacing is generally sufficient for multiple plants.

Where to Plant

Basil performs best with at least eight hours of direct sun each day. Plant basil in rich, well-drained soil, either in the ground or in containers at least 12 inches in diameter or preferably larger. Small containers dry out quickly in Texas's frequent warm temperatures. Ideally, till several inches of organic matter into the soil and incorporate 2 pounds of a complete lawn or garden fertilizer (15-5-10, 13-13-13, and so forth) per 100 square feet of bed or every 35 feet of row. In small plots use 2 teaspoons per square foot or foot of row. The ideal soil pH for growing basil is 5.5 to 7.0.

How to Plant

Basil can be grown either in the ground or containers. I prefer the ground so the plants don't dry out as much. If you are direct seeding, scatter the seed on tilled soil that has been raked smooth. *Gently* rake the seed into the soil, making sure that it is no deeper than ¼ of an inch below the surface of the soil. Water gently and carefully (to avoid disturbing the seed), and keep the soil moist until germination (sprouting) occurs. Then reduce the *frequency* of watering so that the plants gradually get tougher and dry out slightly. Transplants should be placed 18 inches apart in well-cultivated soil. Dig holes that are the same size as the existing pot they are growing in. Gently firm the soil around them, being careful not to plant the transplant any deeper than it was growing in the pot. Water thoroughly with a water-soluble plant food at half the labeled recommendation.

Care and Maintenance

Basil is easy to grow and relatively pest free. To stimulate new tender foliage, keep it trimmed or harvested regularly, keep the flower heads cut off, and apply several teaspoons of a lawn and garden fertilizer (15-5-10, 13-13-13, and so forth) every two to three weeks or a water-soluble fertilizer every one to two weeks.

Harvest

Basil is generally ready to harvest in seventy to eighty days from seed or just weeks from transplants. Harvest basil as young shoots or tender, pest-free leaves that have just reached full size. Wash and use them immediately.

Additional Information

Many different forms of basil perform well in Texas, including 'Genovese', 'Lemon Basil', 'Purple Ruffles', 'Siam Queen', 'Spicy Globe', and 'Sweet Basil'. Basil originated in Asia and Africa.

BEET

Many folks claim not to like beets (*Beta vulgaris*). Heck, I was one of them. Turns out I don't like pickled beets or canned beets. Fresh tender beets from the garden are another story. In addition to the colorful and nutritious roots, the young tops are good as greens and included in many salads. Beets are suited to growing in the fall, mild winters, and spring in most of the state.

When to Plant

Beets are cool-weather plants that die when the weather is hot. For the greens to be tasty and the roots tender, the temperatures must be cool. Beets can tolerate frosts but not hard freezes, so they should be planted in late winter or early spring for an initial crop. A second crop can be planted for fall, around September in the northern half of Texas and in October in the southern half of Texas. Beet seeds are planted directly into the ground. After the seedlings have established themselves and have their first true leaves, thin them to 3 to 4 inches apart.

Where to Plant

Beets require at least eight hours of direct sun each day for maximum yields. Like most root crops, they do best in well-drained sandy and loamy soils, and they are best planted in raised beds or rows at least 6 to 12 inches high. Ideally, till in several inches of compost or organic matter and incorporate 2 pounds of a complete lawn or garden fertilizer (15-5-10, 13-13-13, and so forth) per 100 square feet of bed or every 35 feet of row before planting. In smaller plantings, use 2 teaspoons per square foot or foot of row. The ideal soil pH for growing beets is 6.0 to 7.0.

How to Plant

Beets can be grown either in beds or rows 2 to 3 feet apart. To improve seedling germination (sprouting), soak beet seed in water overnight at room temperature. Open a shallow trench in your raised row 1 inch deep with the corner of a hoe or a stick. Drop the seeds 1 inch apart to ensure a good stand. To prevent the seed from crusting over the sprouting seed, cover with compost or potting soil instead of garden soil. Water gently and carefully (to avoid disturbing the seed), and keep the soil moist until germination occurs. Beet seed may take two to three weeks to sprout in the early spring when the soils are cool but only five to seven days when planted in warmer soils for a fall crop. When the seedlings are up, reduce the *frequency* of watering so that the plants gradually get tougher.

Care and Maintenance

Water and fertility are the most critical issues in growing good beets. Never let them get dry. When the plants are 6 inches tall, fertilize them with ½ cup of high-nitrogen fertilizer (21-0-0, and so forth) for each 35 feet of row. Sprinkle half of the fertilizer down each side of the row. Lightly work it into the soil and then water. The main pest problem on beets is the foliage-feeding flea beetle, which causes numerous small holes in the foliage. Treat with a safe, labeled insecticide as soon as you notice the first damage.

Harvest

Beets are generally ready to harvest in fifty-five to eighty days with greens ready in thirty-five to forty days. For greens, harvest the tender, bug-free foliage when it is less than 6 inches long. For beets, harvest them when they are around 2 inches in diameter. If they are allowed to grow too large, they will be tough and woody. Wash and refrigerate or prepare them immediately after digging.

Additional Information

Recommended beet varieties for Texas include 'Detroit Dark Red', 'Peacemaker II', and 'Ruby Queen'. Beets originated in the Mediterranean.

BROCCOLI

Of course many of us are aware of George H. W. Bush's aversion to this healthy vegetable. He probably never tried a fresh head from his own garden. Nice broccoli (*Brassica oleracea*, Botrytis Group) is easy to grow if you remember that it needs cool weather and high fertility. Many children will eat raw broccoli with assorted tasty dips. In addition, little green cabbage looper worms like to eat broccoli as well. They know what's good, and good for them too.

When to Plant

Broccoli is a cool-weather plant that bolts or flowers and forms seed when the weather is hot. Broccoli can tolerate frosts but not hard freezes, so it should be planted in late winter or early spring for an initial crop. A second fall crop can be planted around September in the northern half of Texas and in October in the southern half of Texas. Broccoli is generally planted as transplants, which are often available from nurseries and garden centers. The transplants should be spaced 12 inches apart.

Where to Plant

Broccoli requires at least eight hours of direct sun each day to perform well. It should be planted in a rich, well-drained soil. Ideally, till several inches of organic matter into the soil and apply 2 pounds of a complete garden fertilizer (15-5-10, 13-13-13, and so forth) per 100 square foot of bed or every 35 feet of row. In small plots use 2 teaspoons per square foot or feet of row. The ideal soil pH for broccoli is 6.0 to 7.0.

How to Plant

Broccoli is almost always transplanted into the garden. Transplants should be placed 12 inches apart in well-cultivated soil. Dig holes that are the same size as the existing pots the broccoli is growing in. Remove from the pots and place the roots into the freshly dug holes. Gently firm the soil around the plants, being careful not to plant them any deeper than they were growing in their pots. Water them thoroughly with a water-soluble plant food such as Miracle-Gro at half the labeled recommendation.

Care and Maintenance

Water and fertility are the most critical issues in growing nice heads of broccoli. Never let them get dry. Two weeks after transplanting, fertilize them with ½ cup of high-nitrogen fertilizer (21-0-0, and so forth) for each 35 feet of row. Sprinkle half of the fertilizer down each side of the row. Lightly work it into the soil and then water. Do this again, using 1 cup of high-nitrogen fertilizer immediately when you notice heads beginning to form. Repeat the same fertilization procedure immediately after the first harvest to stimulate numerous edible side shoots. The main pest problems on broccoli are assorted caterpillars that destroy the foliage. Treat with organic *Bacillus thuringiensis* (*Bt*, Dipel, Thuricide, and so forth) as soon as you notice the first damage. Be on the lookout for aphids as well.

Harvest

Depending on the variety, broccoli is generally ready to pick in sixty to eighty days from transplants. Harvest the heads with a sharp knife when they are tight and compact and around 6 to 8 inches in diameter. As soon as the first buds begin to expand, pick them immediately regardless of the size. Cut the stems 6 to 8 inches below the head. Do not wait until the yellow flowers begin to open. After harvesting the larger head, smaller heads will form from the cut stem of the plant. They are just as tasty and are often easier to prepare.

Additional Information

Recommended broccoli varieties for Texas include 'Baccus', 'Cruiser', 'Emerald Pride', 'Galaxy', 'Green Comet', 'Green Magic', 'Lucky', 'Packman', 'Patron', and 'Premium Crop'. Broccoli is native to the Mediterranean.

BRUSSELS SPROUTS

The episode of the classic television show *Leave It to Beaver*, where the Beaver absolutely refused to eat Brussels Sprouts (*Brassica oleracea*, Gemmifera Group) is burned into my brain. Like most folks who didn't grow up eating their vegetables, he either didn't get started on them soon enough, didn't have a good cook to prepare them (sorry, June Cleaver), or, most likely, never had fresh ones from the garden. It really does make all the difference in the world. Brussels Sprouts need cool temperatures to be sweet and tasty instead of bitter, so make sure to grow them in the fall, in mild winters, and in early spring.

When to Plant

Brussels Sprouts are a cool-weather plant that bolts or goes to seed when the weather is hot. For the mini cabbages to be tender and tasty, the weather must be cool. Brussels Sprouts can tolerate frosts but not hard freezes, so they should be planted in late winter or early spring for an initial crop. A second fall crop can be planted around September in the northern half of Texas, and in October in the southern half of Texas. BrusselsSprouts are generally planted as transplants, which are often available from nurseries and garden centers. The transplants should be spaced 18 inches apart.

Where to Plant

Brussels Sprouts require at least eight hours of direct sun each day. They should be planted in a rich, well-drained soil. Ideally, till several inches of organic matter into the soil and apply 2 pounds of a complete lawn or garden fertilizer (15-5-10, 13-13-13, and so forth) per 100 square feet of bed or every 35 feet of row. In small plots use 2 teaspoons per foot of row or square foot. The ideal soil pH for Brussels Sprouts is 5.5 to 6.5.

How to Plant

Dig holes that are the same size as the existing pot they are growing in. Remove the Brussels Sprouts from the pots and place the roots into the freshly dug holes. Gently firm the soil around them, being careful not to plant the plants any deeper than they were growing in their pots. Water them thoroughly with a liquid plant food at half the labeled recommendation.

Care and Maintenance

Water and fertility are the most critical issues in growing good Brussels Sprouts. Never let them get dry. When the plants are 12 inches tall, fertilize them with 1 cup of high-nitrogen fertilizer (21-0-0, and so forth) for each 35 feet of row. Sprinkle half of the fertilizer down each side of the row. Lightly work it into the soil and then water. The main pest problems on Brussels Sprouts are assorted caterpillars that destroy the foliage. Treat with organic *Bacillus thuringiensis* (*Bt*, Dipel, Thuricide, and so forth) as soon as you notice the first damage. Aphids might also be a problem. If they are, use a safe, appropriately labeled insecticide.

Harvest

Brussels Sprouts are generally ready to start harvesting 90 to 100 days after transplanting. Twist them from the stem, starting at the bottom of the plant when they are 1 to 2 inches in diameter. Wash and refrigerate, or prepare them immediately.

Additional Information

Recommended Brussels Sprouts varieties for Texas include 'Jade Cross' and 'Prince Marvel'. Brussels Sprouts originated in the Mediterranean.

CABBAGE

Cabbage (*Brassica oleracea*, Capitata Group) is a wonderful cool-season vegetable with many uses. My family loves it. At one particular meal, I noticed my dad eating raw cabbage, coleslaw, and cooked cabbage at the same time. Now that's a cabbage lover. Just remember that it requires cool temperatures, high fertility, and diligence to keep the cabbage loopers from enjoying their fair share. After eating your own, you won't want to buy it from the grocery store ever again.

When to Plant

Cabbage is a cool-weather plant that splits and rots when the weather is hot. Its flavor gets stronger with heat as well. For cabbage to be tender and tasty, the weather must be cool. Cabbage can tolerate frosts but not really hard freezes, so it should be planted in late winter or early spring for an initial crop. A second fall crop can be planted around September in the northern half of Texas, and in October in the southern half of Texas. Cabbage is generally planted as transplants, which are often available from nurseries and garden centers. Cabbage transplants should be spaced around 12 inches apart.

Where to Plant

Cabbage requires at least eight hours of direct sun each day to thrive. Plant it in a rich, well-drained soil. Ideally, till several inches of organic matter

into the soil and apply 2 pounds of a complete lawn or garden fertilizer (15-5-10, 13-13-13, and so forth) per 100 square feet of bed or every 35 feet of row. In small plots use 2 teaspoons per square foot or foot of row. The ideal soil pH for cabbage is 5.5 to 6.5.

How to Plant

Dig holes that are the same size as the existing pots in which the cabbage is growing. Remove from the pots and place the roots into the freshly dug holes. Gently firm the soil around them, being careful not to plant the plants any deeper than they were growing in their pots. Water them thoroughly with a water-soluble plant food at half the labeled recommendation.

Care and Maintenance

Water and fertility are the most critical issues in growing nice heads of cabbage. Never let them get dry. Two to three weeks after transplanting, fertilize them with 1 cup of high-nitrogen fertilizer (21-0-0, and so forth) for each 35 feet of row. Sprinkle half of the fertilizer down each side of the row. Lightly work it into the soil and then water. Do this again immediately when you notice heads beginning to form. The main pest problems on cabbage are assorted caterpillars that destroy the foliage. Treat with organic *Bacillus thuringiensis* (*Bt*, Dipel, Thuricide, and so forth) as soon as you notice the first damage. Be on the lookout for aphids as well.

Harvest

Depending on the variety, cabbage is ready to harvest in 65 to 120 days from transplanting. Harvest the heads when they are firm and solid by cutting with a knife or pruners just below the lower leaves. Leave the coarse outer leaves on for protection until you get ready to use the head. Prepare it immediately or refrigerate for up to two weeks. Do not wash before storing because the moisture will cause it to spoil quicker.

Additional Information

Recommended cabbage varieties for Texas include 'Bravo', 'Blue Vantage', 'Early Jersey Wakefield', 'Gourmet', 'Red Rookie', 'Rio Verde', 'Ruby Ball' (red), 'Sanibel', and 'Savoy King' (savoy). Cabbage is native to the Mediterranean.

CANTALOUPE

The aroma of a ripe cantaloupe (*Cucurbita melo*, Reticulatus Group) is almost as good as the taste. And therein lies the problem. If you can't smell a cantaloupe, you probably aren't going to taste it. And to taste a truly luscious one, you'll have to grow and harvest your own when the melon literally slips off the vine without having to be cut. It's a special treat that everyone should enjoy.

When to Plant

Cantaloupe requires warm soils to germinate and is generally planted from seed after all danger of frost in the spring (around April in the northern half of Texas and March in the southern half). Transplants are often available from garden centers as well. Cantaloupe cannot tolerate frosts or freezes. A fall crop of cantaloupe can be planted about four months before the first killing frost. After the seedlings have established themselves and formed their first true leaves, thin them (or plant your transplants), leaving the two strongest plants per hill.

Where to Plant

Cantaloupes require at least eight hours of direct sun each day. They thrive best in loose, sandy soils. Ideally, till in several inches of compost or organic matter and incorporate 2 pounds of a complete lawn or garden fertilizer (15-5-10, 13-13-13, and so forth) per 100 square feet of bed or every 35 feet of row. The ideal soil pH for cantaloupes is 6.0 to 7.5.

How to Plant

Cantaloupe is direct seeded into the garden. Create a raised row about 6 inches high and 12 inches wide. Multiple rows should be around 36 inches apart. Cantaloupe seed should be planted in groups of seed every 5 to 8 feet. This is known as planting in hills. Open a shallow depression about 1 inch deep and 4 inches wide with a hoe. Drop four to five seeds evenly spaced apart in the hole and cover lightly with loose soil using a hoe or garden rake. Tamp the soil down gently with the back of your hoe. Make sure the seed isn't too deep or it won't germinate.

Care and Maintenance

As soon as the vines on the cantaloupe start to run, you need to apply an additional application of fertilizer. This is known as sidedressing. Sprinkle 2 tablespoons of a high-nitrogen fertilizer, such as ammonium sulfate

(21-0-0), around each hill, being careful to keep it off the plants. Work the fertilizer into the soil lightly with a hoe or rake, and water. After side-dressing, it is ideal to apply a layer of organic mulch (hay, straw, grass clippings, and so forth) to conserve water and prevent weeds. Insects and diseases aren't generally a major problem, but be on the lookout for powdery mildew, cucumber beetles, and squash bugs.

Harvest

Most cantaloupe varieties mature about seventy-five to ninety days from seeding. Cantaloupes are harvested when the stem that attaches it to the plant separates or slips from the fruit. If you have to cut it from the plant, it's not ready. Cantaloupes that are picked too early will not be sweet and fragrant.

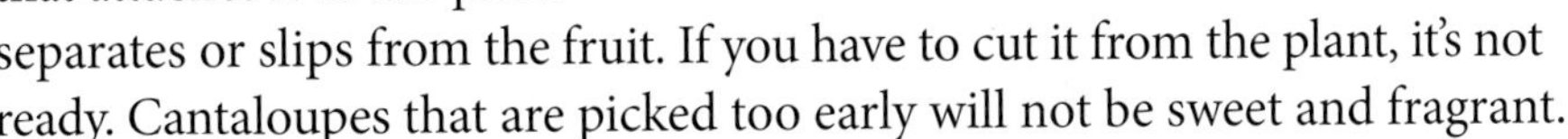

Additional Information

Recommended cantaloupe varieties for Texas include 'Ambrosia', 'Caravelle', 'Cruiser', 'Dixie Jumbo', 'Israeli', 'Magnum 45', 'Mission', 'Perlita', 'Primo', 'TAM Dew', and 'TAM Uvalde'. Cantaloupe probably originated in Persia (Iran) or Africa.

CARROT

The humble carrot (*Daucus carota sativus*) is a vegetable that most folks, even children, will eat—if not cooked, at least raw. I've never seen a child pull a carrot from the ground and not smile and try to eat it before it was even washed. The keys to good-looking carrots are cool temperatures and a loose, friable soil. (Friable soil is a soil texture that crumbles easily in your hands; it's the best kind to have.)

When to Plant

Carrots are cool-weather plants that go to seed when the weather is hot. For the carrots to be tender and sweet, the weather must be cool. Carrots can tolerate frosts but not hard freezes, so they should be planted in late winter or early spring for an initial crop. A fall crop can be planted around September in the northern half of Texas, and in October in the southern half of Texas. Carrots are direct seeded into the garden. After the seedlings have established themselves and formed true leaves, thin them to 1 inch apart. When they get 6 inches tall, thin them to 2 inches apart.

Where to Plant

Carrots require at least eight hours of direct sun each day for maximum yields. Like most root crops, they do best in well-drained sandy and loamy soils and are best planted in raised beds or rows at least 6 to 12 inches high. Ideally, till in several inches of compost or organic matter and incorporate 2 pounds of a complete garden fertilizer (13-13-13, 10-20-10, and so forth)

per 100 square feet of bed or every 35 feet of row before planting. In smaller plantings use 2 teaspoons per square foot or foot of row. The ideal soil pH for growing carrots is 6.5 to 7.5.

How to Plant

Carrots can either be grown in beds or rows 2 to 3 feet apart. Open a shallow trench in your raised row ½ inch deep with the corner of a hoe or a stick. Sow the seeds two to three per inch to ensure a good stand and cover with ¼ to ½ inch of soil. Another option is to sprinkle the seeds on top of the row or bed and lightly rake the surface to cover them. After seeding, gently tamp down the soil with the back of your hoe to ensure good seed-to-soil contact. Water gently and keep the soil moist until germination occurs. Carrot seed may take three weeks to sprout in the early spring but only one week when planted in warmer soils for a fall crop. When the seedlings are up, reduce the *frequency* of watering so that the plants gradually dry out slightly between watering.

Care and Maintenance

Carrots need ideal conditions. Any negative growing conditions—including low light, low fertility, crowded conditions, competition from weeds, or drought—can cause your carrots to be poorly flavored or misshapen. Carrots are not heavy feeders; however, after your final thinning, when they plants are around 6 inches tall, fertilize them with 1 cup of high-nitrogen fertilizer (21-0-0, and so forth) for each 35 feet of row. Sprinkle half of the fertilizer down each side of the row, making sure to keep it off the plants. Lightly work it into the soil and then water. A layer of organic mulch (straw, hay, and so forth) around them is ideal. Unfortunately, most of the carrot's pest problems are underground, and you won't know you have them until after harvest.

Harvest

Full-sized carrots should be ready to harvest 70 to 100 days after planting, although carrots of any size can be harvested at any time. Always pull the biggest carrots first.

Additional Information

Recommended carrot varieties for Texas include 'Danvers 126', 'Imperator 58', 'Nantes', 'Orlando Gold', 'Purple Dragon', 'Spartan Winner', and 'Texas Gold Spike'. In addition to orange, carrots can be white, yellow, red, or purple. Carrots originated in Afghanistan.

CAULIFLOWER

Cauliflower (*Brassica oleracea*, Botrytis Group) balances out being healthy and nutritious by being a bit difficult to grow. Be very aware that this cool-season crop can't take very much heat or cold. It's possible to grow a successful crop in the spring and again in the fall if you use transplants and pay attention to the proper planting dates in your area.

When to Plant

Cauliflower is a cool-weather plant that bolts or goes to seed when the weather is hot. Its flavor gets stronger with heat as well. Cauliflower can tolerate frosts but not hard freezes, so it should be planted in late winter or early spring for an initial crop. A second fall crop can be planted around September in the northern half of Texas, and in October in the southern half of Texas. Cauliflower is generally planted as transplants, which are often available from nurseries and garden centers. The transplants should be planted 15 to 18 inches apart.

Where to Plant

Cauliflower requires at least eight hours of direct sun each day. It should be planted in a rich, well-drained soil. Ideally, till in several inches of organic matter and apply 2 pounds of a complete lawn or garden fertilizer (15-5-10, 13-13-13, and so forth) per 100 square feet of bed or every 35 feet of row. In small plots use 2 teaspoons per square foot or foot of row. The ideal soil pH for growing cauliflower is 6.0 to 7.0.

How to Plant

Dig holes that are the same size as the existing pot the cauliflower is growing in. Remove from the pots and place the roots into the freshly dug holes. Gently firm the soil around them, being careful not to plant the plants any deeper than they were growing in their pots. Water them thoroughly with a water-soluble food such as Miracle-Gro at half the labeled recommendation.

Care and Maintenance

Water and fertility are the most critical issues in growing nice heads of cauliflower. Never let them get dry. Four to six weeks after transplanting, fertilize them with 1 cup of high-nitrogen fertilizer (21-0-0, and so forth) for each 35 feet of row. Sprinkle half of the fertilizer down each side of the row. Lightly work it into the soil and then water. In order to produce white, tender heads of cauliflower, you will want to blanch them. When you first

notice the small head starting to form in the middle of the plant, tie the larger outer leaves together in the middle of the plant using garden twine. Any amount of light that shines on the forming heads will discolor them, but they will still be edible. The main pest problems on cauliflower are assorted caterpillars that destroy the foliage. Treat with organic *Bacillus thuringiensis* (*Bt,* Dipel, Thuricide, and so forth) as soon as you notice the first damage. Be on the lookout for aphids as well.

Harvest

Depending on the variety, cauliflower is generally ready to harvest fifty-five to seventy-five days from transplanting. Cauliflower is ready to harvest when the curds (immature flower buds) are firm, compact, and relatively smooth. Under ideal conditions the heads will be 6 to 8 inches in diameter. Do not wait until the curds start to separate.

Additional Information

Recommended cauliflower varieties for Texas include 'Snow Ball Improved', 'Snow Crown', and 'Snow King'. Cauliflower originated in the Mediterranean.

CILANTRO

This traditional Tex-Mex herb is also known as coriander or Chinese parsley and is used in ethnic cooking throughout the world. Cilantro (*Coriandrum sativum*) is a cool-season annual that must be grown during the spring, fall, and mild winters in Texas. If it is allowed to go to seed during the summer, you will be rewarded with a self-sown volunteer crop when the cooler temperatures and moisture of autumn arrives.

When to Plant

Cilantro is a cool-weather plant that bolts or goes to seed when the weather is hot. Its flavor gets stronger with heat as well. For cilantro to be tender and tasty, the weather must be mild. Cilantro can tolerate frosts but not hard freezes, so it should be planted in late winter or early spring for an initial crop. A second fall crop can be planted around September in the northern half of Texas, and in October in the southern half of Texas. Cilantro can either be direct seeded or planted as transplants, which are often available from nurseries and garden centers. After the seedlings have established themselves and formed their first true leaves, thin them to 4 inches apart (or plant your transplants 4 inches apart).

Where to Plant

Cilantro requires at least eight hours of direct sun each day. It should be planted in rich, well-drained soil, either in the ground or in containers at

least 12 inches in diameter, preferably larger. Small containers dry out quickly in frequent warm temperatures. Ideally, till several inches of organic matter into the soil and incorporate 2 pounds of a complete lawn or garden fertilizer (15-5-10, 13-13-13, and so forth) per 100 square feet of bed or every 35 feet of row. In small plots use 2 teaspoons per square foot or foot of row. The ideal pH for growing cilantro is 6.0 to 7.0.

How to Plant

If you are direct seeding, scatter cilantro seed on tilled soil that has been raked smooth. Gently rake the seed into the soil, making sure that it is no deeper than ¼ of an inch below the surface of the soil. Water gently and carefully (to avoid disturbing the seed), and keep the soil moist until germination (sprouting) occurs. Then reduce the *frequency* of watering so that the plants gradually get tougher. Transplants should be planted in holes dug the same size as the existing pot they are growing in. Gently firm the soil around them, being careful not to plant the transplant any deeper than it was growing in the pot. Water thoroughly with a water-soluble plant food at half the labeled recommendation.

Care and Maintenance

Cilantro is easy to grow and relatively pest free. To stimulate new tender foliage, keep it trimmed or harvested regularly, keep the flower heads cut off, and apply several teaspoons of a lawn and garden fertilizer (15-5-10, 13-13-13, and so forth) every two to three weeks or a water-soluble fertilizer every one to two weeks.

Harvest

Cilantro is generally ready to harvest thirty-five to forty-five days from seeding. Harvest tender pest-free leaves that have just reached full size. Wash and use them immediately.

Additional Information

Recommended cilantro varieties for Texas include 'Santo', 'Leisure', 'Delfino', and 'Confetti'. Cilantro is native to the Mediterranean.

COLLARDS

When I was studying horticulture at Texas A&M University, I remember the effervescent Dr. Joe Novak teaching us about the nutritional content of different vegetables. While he rambled on at 90 miles an hour, I quietly ranked each vegetable in the different vitamin and nutritional categories. It turns out that the most nutritious vegetable of all isn't spinach or broccoli as commonly touted, but collards (*Brassica oleracea*, Acephala Group) and their twin, kale. This cool-season green is a staple in the rural South but should be incorporated into everybody's garden and diet.

When to Plant

Collard greens are cool-weather plants that bolt or go to seed when the weather is extremely hot. The flavor gets stronger with heat as well. And like most greens, the texture gets tougher with the onset of warm weather. Collard greens can tolerate frosts and moderate freezes but not very hard freezes, so they should be planted in late winter or early spring for an initial crop. A second fall crop can be planted around September in the northern half of Texas and in October in the southern half of Texas. Collards are generally planted as transplants, which are often available from nurseries and garden centers. They should be planted 18 inches apart.

Where to Plant

Collard greens require at least eight hours of direct sun each day, but like most greens they can tolerate a bit of filtered light, or as little as five to six hours of direct sun. Just remember that any amount of shade reduces production and makes the leaves larger and thinner. Plant collards in a rich, well-drained soil. Ideally, till in several inches of organic matter and incorporate 2 pounds of a complete lawn or garden fertilizer (15-5-10, 13-13-13, and so forth) per 100 square feet of bed or every 35 feet of row. In small plots use 2 teaspoons per square foot or foot of row. The ideal soil pH for growing collards is 6.0 to 7.0.

How to Plant

Dig holes in well-cultivated soil that are the same size as the existing pots the transplants are growing in. Remove from the pots and place the roots into the freshly dug holes. Gently firm the soil around them, being careful not to plant the plants any deeper than they were growing in their pots. Water them thoroughly with a water-soluble plant food such as Miracle-Gro at half the labeled recommendation.

Care and Maintenance

Collards are relatively easy to grow. For the best flavor and production, they require cool temperatures and high fertility. Two to three weeks after transplanting, fertilize them with 1 cup of high-nitrogen fertilizer (21-0-0, and so forth) for each 35 feet of row. Sprinkle half of the fertilizer down each side of the row. Lightly work it into the soil and then water. Repeat this fertilizing process every three to four weeks to encourage high yields. The main pest problems on collards are assorted caterpillars that destroy the foliage. Treat with organic *Bacillus thuringiensis* (*Bt,* Dipel, Thuricide, and so forth) as soon as you notice the first damage.

Harvest

Collard greens are generally ready to harvest three to four weeks after planting transplants. Pick the lower, pest-free leaves that have just reached full size but are still tender. Wash and prepare or refrigerate immediately.

Additional Information

Recommended collard varieties for Texas include 'Blue Max', 'Champion', 'Georgia Southern', and 'Vates'. Collards are native to the Mediterranean.

CUCUMBER

I come from a family of pickle eaters, so I've been growing cucumbers (*Cucumis sativus*) for most of my life. In Texas, cucumbers must be grown during the cooler months of spring and early summer, as they turn bitter and die during hot summers. As with most Texas spring vegetable crops, it's possible to grow another cup of cucumbers in the fall as well. Cucumber varieties are separated into slicing types and pickling types.

When to Plant

Cucumbers require warm soils to germinate and should be planted after all danger of frost in the spring (generally April in the northern half of Texas and March in the southern half). They cannot tolerate frost or freezes. A fall crop of cucumbers can be planted about four months before the first killing frost. Cucumbers can be planted from seed or transplants that are often available from nurseries and garden centers. Once the seedlings are established and have their true leaves, they should be thinned to (or transplants planted) 2 to 3 feet apart.

Where to Plant

Cucumbers perform best with at least eight hours of direct sun each day. The plants aren't picky about soils as long as they drain well. Ideally, till in several inches of compost or organic matter and incorporate 2 pounds of a complete lawn or garden fertilizer (15-5-10, 13-13-13, and so forth) per 100 square feet of bed or every 35 feet of row before planting. For smaller

plots, use 2 teaspoons per square foot or foot of row. The ideal soil pH for growing cucumbers is 5.5 to 7.0

How to Plant

Cucumbers are generally direct seeded into the garden. Create a raised row about 6 inches high and 12 inches wide. Multiple rows should be around 36 inches apart. Cucumber seed should be planted in groups of seed every 5 to 8 feet. This is known as planting in hills. Open a shallow depression about 1 to 1⅕ inches deep and 4 inches wide with a hoe. Drop four to six seeds evenly spaced apart in the hole and cover lightly with loose soil using a hoe or garden rake. Gently tamp the soil down with the back of the hoe. Make sure the seed isn't too deep or it won't germinate.

Care and Maintenance

I prefer to grow my cucumbers on wire fence trellises for cleaner and straighter fruit. As soon as the vines on the cucumbers start to run or climb, you need to apply an additional application of fertilizer. This is known as sidedressing. Sprinkle 2 tablespoons of a high-nitrogen fertilizer, such as ammonium sulfate (21-0-0), around each hill, being careful to keep it off the plants. Work the fertilizer into the soil lightly with a hoe or rake, and water. After side-dressing, applying a layer of organic mulch (hay, straw, grass clippings, and so forth) to conserve water and prevent weeds is ideal. Insects and diseases aren't generally a major problem, but be on the lookout for cucumber beetles, leaf miners, and squash bugs.

Harvest

Depending on the variety, cucumbers are generally ready to harvest fifty-five to sixty days from seeding. Always pick every fruit that is of usable size. Leaving a single fruit on the plant too long will cause the plant to cease production. Tender smaller-sized cucumbers are the best. There is no such thing as one too small to use. However, very large, seedy cucumbers that look like small watermelons are not something to be proud of or gifted to friends and neighbors. They should be deposited in the compost pile or fed to the nearest horse.

Additional Information

Recommended cucumber varieties for Texas include 'Burpless' (slicing), 'Dasher II' (slicing), 'Poinsett 76' (slicing), 'Straight Eight' (slicing), 'Sweet Slice' (slicing), 'Sweet Success' (slicing), 'Carolina' (pickling), and 'Calypso' (pickling). Cucumbers originated in India.

DILL

Although traditionally served on new potatoes, this tangy herb is most known for flavoring dill pickles. It's important to plant your dill (*Anethum graveolens*) from transplants long before planting your cucumbers to ensure you will have a plentiful supply for your pickling projects. It's a cool-season plant that won't tolerate the heat of summer, so it must be grown during the fall, mild winters, and spring in Texas.

When to Plant

Dill is a cool-weather plant that bolts or goes to seed when the weather is hot. For dill to be vigorous and tender, the weather must be cool. Dill can tolerate frosts but not hard freezes, so it should be planted in late winter or early spring for an initial crop. A second fall crop can be planted when summer is wrapping up, around September in the northern half of Texas and October in the southern half of Texas. Dill is generally planted as transplants, which are often available from nurseries and garden centers. The transplants should be planted 10 to 12 inches apart.

Where to Plant

Dill requires at least eight hours of direct sun each day. It should be planted in loamy, well-drained soil, either in the ground or in containers at least 12 inches in diameter or preferably larger. Small containers dry out quickly in Texas's frequent warm temperatures, leading to plant death or stress. Ideally, till several inches of organic matter into the soil and apply 2 pounds of a complete lawn or garden fertilizer (15-5-10, 13-13-13, and so forth) per 100 square feet of bed or every 35 feet of row. In small plots, use 2 teaspoons per square foot or foot of row. The ideal soil pH for growing dill is 6.0 to 7.0.

How to Plant

Dig holes that are the same size as the existing pot the plants are growing in. Gently firm the soil around them, being careful not to plant the transplant any deeper than it was growing in the pot. Water thoroughly with a water-soluble plant food such as Miracle-Gro at half the labeled recommendation.

Care and Maintenance

Dill is relatively easy to grow. To promote new shoots and foliage, pick leaves and flower or seed heads regularly, and apply several teaspoons of a lawn and garden fertilizer (15-5-10, 13-13-13, and so forth) every two to three weeks or a water-soluble fertilizer every one to two weeks. The main pest to look out for is the larva (caterpillar) of the beautiful eastern black

swallowtail butterfly. Many gardeners leave them alone and plant extra dill to share.

Harvest

Dill is generally ready to harvest three to four weeks from transplanting. Harvest tender pest-free leaves that have just reached full size. Flower and immature seed heads may also be harvested and used. Wash and use them immediately. All parts of the dill plant may be dried for later use.

Additional Information

Recommended dill varieties for Texas include 'Dukat', 'Long Island Mammoth', and 'Diana'. If you let your dill go to seed, ripen, dry, and shatter (fall to the ground), you'll be rewarded with a volunteer crop of seedlings. Dill is native to Eurasia.

EGGPLANT

I think more Texas gardeners would grow eggplant (*Solanum melongena*) if they understood its need for mild spring conditions instead of hot summer temperatures. When temperatures get over 85 degrees, eggplant fruits become bitter. In this case bitter is "badder." It wouldn't hurt to pass around some good recipes that use eggplants either. Eggplant is related to tomatoes, peppers, and potatoes, and has been grown and consumed in India and Asia for thousands of years. Eggplant can be purple, green, or white, as well as fat and round, or long and skinny. Surely one of them will fit at your table.

When to Plant

Eggplant is planted from transplants in the spring, after all danger of frost has passed. It thrives with mild and moderately warm temperatures but cannot tolerate a frost or freeze. Hot temperatures will make eggplant fruits taste bitter. Often summer heat and drought kill spring-planted eggplants in Texas. By planting transplants again four months before the first expected killing freeze in your area, you can successfully grow a fall crop. Eggplant transplants should be spaced 24 inches apart.

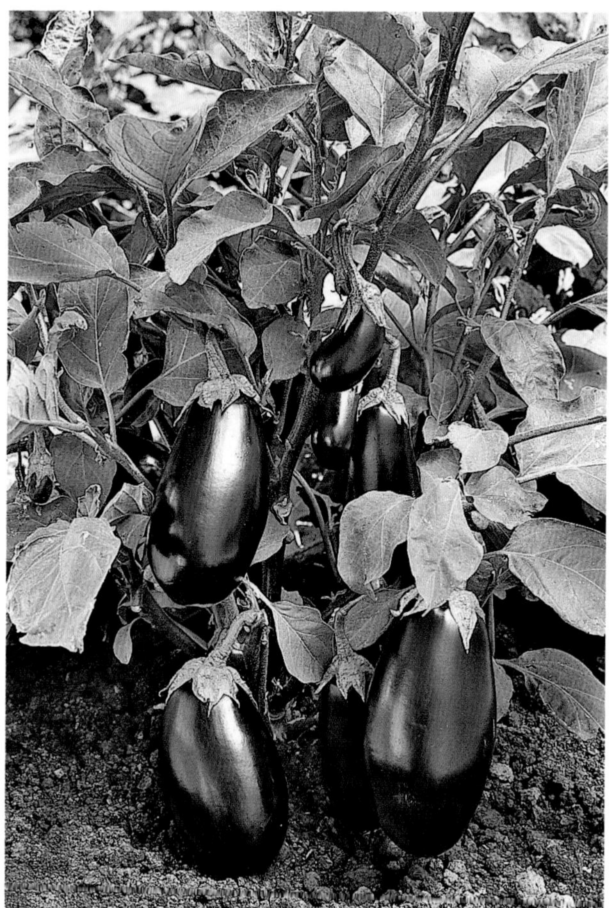

Where to Plant

Eggplant requires at least eight hours of direct sun each day to do well. It performs best in a rich, loamy soil that drains well. Ideally, till in several inches of compost or organic matter and incorporate 2 pounds of a complete lawn or garden fertilizer (15-5-10, 13-13-13, and so forth) per 100 square feet of bed or every 35 feet of row before planting. Use 2 teaspoons per square foot or foot of row for small plantings. The ideal soil pH for growing eggplant is 6.0 to 7.0

How to Plant

Eggplant transplants should be planted in well-cultivated soil. Dig holes that are the same size as the existing pot they are growing in. Gently firm the soil around them, being careful not to plant the transplants any deeper than they were growing in the pot. Water thoroughly with a water-soluble plant food at half the labeled recommendation.

Care and Maintenance

Eggplants grow and set fruit best when the temperatures are mild. About three weeks after transplanting, fertilize them with 1 cup of high nitrogen fertilizer (21-0-0, and so forth) for each 35 feet of row. Sprinkle half the fertilizer down each side of the row. Lightly work it into the soil and then water. Repeat this fertilizing process every three weeks to keep the plants vigorous. The main pest problems on eggplant are flea beetles, leaf miners, potato bugs, and spider mites. Treat with an appropriately labeled insecticide when you notice the first damage. Cut off misshapen fruit so the plant will use the energy on new fruit.

Harvest

Depending on the variety, eggplant will be ready for harvesting seventy to ninety days from transplanting. The fruits can be harvested at any size, but are normally picked when they reach about two-thirds maximum size, aren't tough, and don't have hard seed. When you press on the side of the eggplant with your thumb, it should spring back with just a slight impression. Eggplant stems are tough, so you'll need to harvest them with pruning shears or a sharp knife.

Additional Information

Recommended eggplant varieties for Texas include 'Black Beauty', 'Ichiban', 'Florida Market', 'Florida High Bush', 'Midnight', 'Tycoon', 'Long Green', and 'Imperial'. Large-fruited eggplants originated in India.

ENGLISH PEA

English peas (*Pisum sativum*) aren't a common vegetable in Texas. But since lots of folks move here from the North and want to grow them, they are in this book. Growing them successfully is fairly difficult (but not impossible), as these true peas can't take extreme cold or much heat. That only leaves a small window of opportunity here to get the job done.

When to Plant

English peas are cool-weather plants that die when the weather is hot. They can tolerate frosts but not hard freezes and are best adapted as a fall crop in Texas, planted eight to ten weeks before the first freeze is expected. Growing English peas as a spring crop in Texas is very difficult due to rapidly warming temperatures. In mild, southern areas of the state, they can be planted in midwinter for a risky spring harvest. English peas are almost always direct seeded into the garden. When the pea seedlings are up and established (about a week), the dwarf types should be thinned to 2 to 3 inches apart and the climbing types to 5 inches apart.

Where to Plant

English peas require at least eight hours of direct sun each day. They aren't terribly picky about soil types but should be planted in areas that drain well. Ideally, till several inches of compost or organic matter into the soil if possible and incorporate 1 pound of a complete garden fertilizer (13-13-13, 10-20-10, and so forth) per 100 square feet of bed or every 35 feet of row. The ideal soil pH for growing green English peas is 6.5 to 7.5.

How to Plant

Create a raised row about 6 inches high and 16 to 24 inches wide. Multiple rows should be around 30 to 48 inches apart. Open a shallow trench 1 to 1½ inches deep with the corner of a hoe or a stick. Drop the seed several inches apart to ensure a good stand. Cover lightly with loose soil using a hoe or garden rake. Make sure the seed isn't too deep or it won't germinate.

Care and Maintenance

It is important to keep your English peas regularly watered. When the soil is dry 1 inch below the surface, water until it's wet to a depth of 6 to 8 inches. Applying an organic mulch of compost, straw, or grass clippings will help conserve moisture, stabilize the soil temperature, and prevent weeds. Avoid excessive fertilizing, which will lead to unnecessary foliage growth and

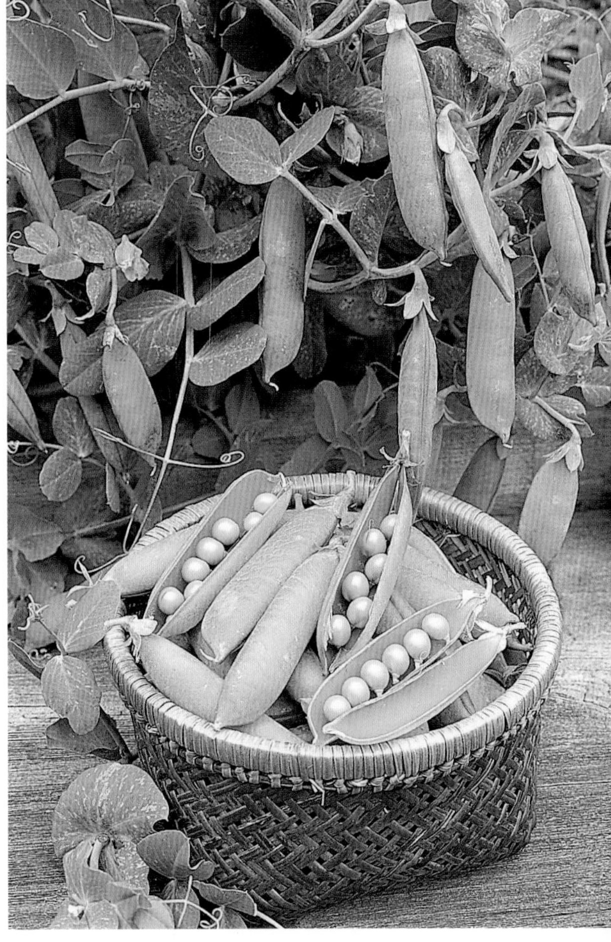

delayed flowering. All true peas have a desire to climb. The dwarf types will twine upon themselves; however, the climbing types will need cattle panels, chicken wire, concrete reinforcing wire, or snow fencing to climb on. Luckily, insects and diseases are not a major problem. Unfortunately, heat, drought, and excessive cold are.

Harvest

Depending on the variety, English peas are ready to harvest sixty to seventy days after planting. Harvest English peas for shelling when the pods appear plump and the peas are full sized but still tender. Pick edible podded peas when the pods are full sized yet still tender with the peas inside the size of BBs. Hold the vine just below the pod with one hand and pull the pod with the other to avoid damaging the vine. Harvest the peas just before cooking, as the sugar in them is rapidly converted to starch and they won't be as tasty.

Additional Information

Recommended English pea varieties for Texas include 'Alaska', 'Knight', 'Little Marvel', 'Progress No. 9', 'Wando', 'Early Snap' (edible podded), 'Sugar Ann' (edible podded), 'Sugar Bon' (edible podded), and 'Sugar Snap' (edible podded). Peas are considered the world's oldest vegetable and were first cultivated by the Chinese 5,000 years ago.

FIELD CORN

Throughout the rural South, folks traditionally grew field corn (*Zea mays*) for feeding their livestock and families. It was harvested dried and stored in log corncribs. Fresh ears would be picked and enjoyed as roasting ears, while the dried corn would be fed to the cows, pigs, horses, and chickens. In addition it was ground into meal for cornbread, corn pone, hoecakes, hush puppies, spoon bread, cush cush, thickening, and batter for catfish, okra, and other Southern delicacies. With the price of corn these days, it makes sense to grow your own.

When to Plant

Field corn is a warm-season plant that cannot tolerate frosts or freezes. It should be planted as soon as possible after the last frost in your region but not before. Planting too soon while the soils are cold will result in rotted seed. However, if you wait too long after the last frost, you will most likely have to deal with dry conditions and a poor harvest. Field corn is easily planted from seed. Once the seedlings are established, thin them to 12 inches apart.

Where to Plant

Field corn requires at least eight hours of direct sun each day for maximum production. Like most grains, field corn isn't picky about soils as long as

they drain well. Ideally, till in several inches of compost or organic matter and incorporate 2 pounds of a complete lawn or garden fertilizer (15-5-10, 13-13-13, and so forth) per 100 square feet of bed or every 35 feet of row before planting. The ideal soil pH for growing field corn is 6.0 to 7.0.

How to Plant

Field corn seed is generally planted 1 to 1½ inches deep in rows that are 30 to 42 inches apart with the seeds 3 to 4 inches apart.

Care and Maintenance

Field corn is a grass and fairly easy to grow if you follow the basic rules of growing grass. It requires regular moisture of about 1 inch of water per week. It also requires high fertility so it's important to apply additional high-nitrogen fertilizer (21-0-0, and so forth) several times during the growth of the plant for maximum production. Use about ½ cup per 35 feet of row, sprinkled lightly down each side of the row. Do not get it on the plant, however. This should be done when the plants are about 6 inches high and again at about waist high, or half grown. It's important that field corn foliage be dark green, never yellow-green, which indicates poor nutrition. The main pest of field corn is the corn earworm, which will eat the kernels off the top of the ear while inside the husk. They can be controlled by regularly keeping *Bacillus thuringiensis* (*Bt,* Dipel, Thuricide) sprinkled or sprayed on the plants and ears.

Harvest

For roasting ears, pick ears that feel full in the shucks and have silks that are golden brown to medium brown. If left on the plant until the shucks completely dry to a dark brown color, the corn will be tough and starchy. Cook and serve immediately for the best flavor. For dried corn for meal and feed, leave the ears on the stalk until both the ears and stalks are completely dried. The kernels will be hard and solid and can then be stored or shelled.

Additional Information

Recommended field corn varieties for Texas include 'Hickory King', 'Pencil Cob', 'Truckers Favorite', and 'Reid's Yellow Dent'. Field corn originated in South America.

GARLIC

Garlic (*Allium sativum*) has been produced and eaten for thousands of years in many cultures. Throughout those years, it was famous for providing strength, warding off evil spirits and vampires, curing ailments, and flavoring foods. Cooking today wouldn't be the same without garlic. This cool-season perennial plant is easy to grow and should be in every garden. There are many varieties to choose from. I suggest swapping for a start from somebody you know to ensure that it's a selection that does well in your area.

When to Plant

Garlic is a cool-season plant that bolts or goes to flower when the weather is warm. In order for garlic to produce enough foliage to store up energy for next year's bulbs, the weather must be cool. Garlic is planted in the fall from bulb segments called cloves. The cloves should be planted 4 inches apart.

Where to Plant

Garlic requires at least eight hours of direct sun each day for maximum yields. Like most root crops, it does best in well-drained sandy and loamy soils and is best planted in raised beds or rows at least 6 to 12 inches high. Ideally, till in several inches of compost or organic matter and incorporate 1 pound of a complete lawn or garden fertilizer (15-5-10, 13-13-13, and so forth) per 100 square feet of bed or every 35 feet of row before planting. In smaller plantings use 1 teaspoon per square foot or foot of row. The ideal soil pH for growing garlic is 6.0 to 7.0.

How to Plant

Garlic can be grown in raised beds or raised rows 6 inches high, 18 inches wide, and 36 inches apart. Use a stick or hoe handle to poke holes into the soil 2 inches deep. Separate the cloves from the garlic bulb and place one clove, pointed side up, into each hole. Gently cover with well-cultivated soil and lightly tamp down with the back of a hoe and water.

Care and Maintenance

Garlic is relatively easy to grow, provided it has lots of sunshine and cool temperatures. Around three to four weeks after planting, or when the plants are 6 inches tall, fertilize them with 1 cup of high-nitrogen fertilizer (21-0-0, and so forth) for each 35 feet of row. Sprinkle half of the fertilizer down each side of the row. Lightly work it into the soil and then water. When cultivating, be careful not to damage the base of the plant. Hand weeding

around the plants is best. After side-dressing with fertilizer, applying a layer of organic mulch (hay, straw, grass clippings, and so forth) to conserve water and prevent weeds is ideal.

Harvest

When the tops dry and fall over (usually early summer), garlic is ready to be harvested. Using a spading fork, gently lift the entire plants from the ground and allow them to dry for a few days in a shady area. Then cut the tops off, leaving about 1 inch above the bulb. Store them in a cool, dry area.

Additional Information

Recommended garlic varieties for Texas are the soft-necked types, including 'California Early', 'Elephant', 'Lorz Italian', 'Mexican Pink', 'Mild French', 'Nootka Rose', 'Siciliana', 'Silverwhite', and 'Texas White'. The large, mild-tasting elephant garlic isn't a true garlic, but a leek instead. Garlic originated in Eurasia.

GREEN BEAN

My oldest brother, Doice, used to gag and sputter and refuse to eat green beans (*Phaseolus vulgaris*) as a child. I'll be the first to admit that those mushy things out of a can weren't my favorite either. I remember they tasted better than a spanking though. Imagine my surprise when I started growing them myself and found out how much better *any* fresh vegetable was than a canned one. To this day I hardly eat any canned vegetable. Why would you when you can grow them much better in your garden?

When to Plant

Green beans require warm soils to germinate and should be planted after all danger of frost in the spring (April in the northern half of Texas and March in the southern half). Planting too soon while the soils are cold will result in poor germination and stunted plants. However, if you wait too long after the last frost, you will most likely have to deal with dry conditions and a poor harvest. A fall crop of green beans can be planted at least three months before the first killing frost. Just remember that green beans form best when the temperatures are in the 70s. After the seedlings establish themselves and have their first true leaves, thin the plants to 3 to 4 inches apart.

Where to Plant

Green beans require at least eight hours of direct sun each day. Beans aren't terribly picky about soil types but should be planted in areas that drain well. Ideally, till several inches of compost or organic matter into the soil if

possible and incorporate 2 pounds of a complete garden fertilizer (13-13-13, 10-20-10, and so forth) per 100 square feet of bed or every 35 feet of row. The ideal soil pH for growing green beans is 6.0 to 7.5.

How to Plant

Green beans are direct seeded into the garden. Create a raised row about 6 inches high and 8 to 12 inches wide. Multiple rows should be around 36 inches apart. Open a shallow trench 1 to 1½ inches deep with the corner of a hoe or a stick. Drop the seed several inches apart to ensure a good stand. Cover lightly with loose soil using a hoe or garden rake. Make sure the seed isn't too deep or it won't germinate.

Care and Maintenance

Check the progress of your green bean plants when they are 6 to 8 inches tall. If they are vigorous and healthy, you don't need to do a thing. If they are pale green and not vigorous, you will need to apply a high-nitrogen fertilizer to stimulate their growth. Use 1 cup of ammonium sulfate (21-0-0) for every 35 feet of row. Sprinkle half of the fertilizer down each side of the row. Lightly work it into the soil and then water. This extra fertilizer application to boost the plants along is known as sidedressing. Green beans are relatively pest free; however, watch for aphids, stinkbugs, spider mites, and rust, and treat with a safe, labeled pesticide.

Harvest

Green beans are generally ready to harvest about fifty-six days from seeding. Green beans should be harvested when the pods are young and tender, 3 to 5 inches long, and before the seeds inside begin to bulge. It's better to pick them too small than too large. Harvest them at least every other day so the pods don't become tough and stringy.

Additional Information

Recommended varieties for Texas include 'Blue Lake' (round), 'Contender' (round), 'Derby' (round), 'Tendergreen' (round), 'Topcrop' (round), 'Blue Lake-Pole' (round), 'Jade-Pole' (round), 'Kentucky Wonder-Pole' (round), 'Greencrop' (flat), 'Roma II' (flat), and 'Purple Podded' Pole (flat). Green beans are native to Central America.

HOT PEPPER

Most Texans grew up eating Tex-Mex food and have a built-in taste for hot peppers (*Capsicum annuum*). Hot peppers are heat tolerant, easy to grow, and widely available. As we all know, depending on the variety, they range from mildly hot to wildly hot. We all have friends with mouths of steel who can eat them all, but particularly like to show off with those that start fires. Once my grandfather reached down and touched a spider on the floor with a hot pepper he was eating. We all watched in disbelief as the spider withered under the heat. My Papaw smiled and kept eating. Fresh hot peppers make good eating for those who can stand it and are great for cooking and flavoring for those who need just a little spice in their lives.

When to Plant

Hot peppers are planted from transplants after all danger of frost in the spring. They cannot tolerate a frost or a freeze and thrive with mild and moderately warm temperatures in spring and early summer. Often summer heat and drought kill spring-planted hot peppers in Texas. By planting transplants again four months before the first expected killing freeze in your area, you can successfully grow a fall crop.

Where to Plant

Hot peppers do best with at least eight hours of direct sun each day. Peppers grow best in rich, loamy soils that drain well. Ideally, till in several inches of compost or organic matter and incorporate 2 pounds of a complete lawn or garden fertilizer (15-5-10, 13-13-13, and so forth) per 100 square feet of bed or every 35 feet of row before planting. For smaller plots, use 2 teaspoons per square foot or foot of row. The ideal soil pH for growing hot peppers is 6.0 to 7.0.

How to Plant

Hot pepper transplants should be planted in well-cultivated soil. Dig holes that are the same size as the existing pots they are growing in. Gently firm the soil around them and water thoroughly with a water-soluble plant food such as Miracle-Gro at half the labeled recommendation.

Care and Maintenance

Hot peppers grow and produce fruit best when the temperatures are warm but below 90 degrees. About three weeks after transplanting, fertilize them with 1 cup of high-nitrogen fertilizer (21-0-0, and so forth) for each 35 feet of row. Sprinkle half of the fertilizer down each side of the row. Lightly work it into the soil and then water. Repeat this fertilizing process every

three weeks to keep the plants vigorous. The main pest problems on peppers are leaf miners, spider mites, nematodes, and foliage diseases. If they occur, treat with an appropriately labeled pesticide.

Harvest

Depending on the variety, you should pick hot peppers 65 to 80 days after transplanting them into the garden. Hot peppers can be harvested at any size but are most pungent and flavorful when they reach full maturity and their normal mature color. Be careful picking the peppers, as the plants are brittle and prone to breaking off. It's actually best to cut the peppers from the plant with a sharp knife or hand pruners. Wash, prepare, or refrigerate them immediately.

Additional Information

Recommended hot pepper varieties for Texas include 'Big Jim', 'Cayenne', 'Chile Pequin', 'Habanero', 'Hungarian Wax', 'Jalapeño', 'Serrano', 'TAMU Hidalgo Serrano', 'TAM Mild Jalapeño', and 'Tabasco'. Hot peppers are native to Central and South America.

KALE

Kale (*Brassica oleracea*, Acephala Group) is botanically the same thing as collards. While collard greens are associated with the American South, kale is more associated with Eastern Europe. Collards have smooth, rounded leaves while kale has either highly crinkled leaves or heavily cut or dissected leaves. In addition to typical green, kale can be colored with white, pink, or purple. No matter its color, kale is one of the most nutritious vegetables for you on the planet and should be incorporated into as many dishes as possible.

When to Plant

Kale is a cool-weather plant that bolts or goes to seed when the weather is extremely hot. The flavor gets stronger with heat as well. And like most greens, the texture gets tougher with warm weather. Kale can tolerate frosts and moderate freezes but not very hard freezes, so it should be planted in late winter or early spring for an initial crop. A second fall crop can be planted around September in the northern half of Texas and in October in the southern half of Texas. Kale is generally planted from transplants, which are often available from nurseries and garden centers. They should be planted 12 inches apart.

Where to Plant

Kale requires at least eight hours of direct sun each day, but like most leafy greens it can tolerate a bit of filtered light, or as little as five to six hours of direct sun. Just remember that any amount of shade reduces production. Plant kale in a rich, well-drained soil or in a large container at least 12 inches in diameter or preferably larger. Small containers dry out quickly in Texas's frequent warm

temperatures. Ideally, till several inches of organic matter into the soil and apply 2 pounds of a complete lawn or garden fertilizer (15-5-10, 13-13-13, and so forth) per 100 square feet of bed or every 35 feet of row. In small plots use 2 teaspoons per square foot or foot of row. The ideal soil pH for growing kale is 6.0 to 7.0.

How to Plant

Dig holes that are the same size as the existing pots the kale is growing in. Remove from the pots and place the roots into the freshly dug holes. Gently firm the soil around them, being careful not to plant the plants any deeper than they were growing in their pots. Water them thoroughly with a water-soluble plant food at half the labeled recommendation.

Care and Maintenance

Kale is relatively easy to grow. For the best flavor and production, it requires cool temperatures and high fertility. Two to three weeks after transplanting, fertilize the plants with 1 cup of high-nitrogen fertilizer (21-0-0, and so forth) for each 35 feet of row. Sprinkle half of the fertilizer down each side of the row. Lightly work it into the soil and then water. Repeat this fertilizing process every three to four weeks to encourage high yields. The main pest problems on kale are assorted caterpillars that destroy the foliage. Treat with organic *Bacillus thuringiensis* (*Bt,* Dipel, Thuricide, and so forth) as soon as you notice the first damage.

Harvest

Depending on the variety, kale is generally ready to harvest in forty-five to fifty-five days from seeding or in half that time from transplants. Pick the lower insect-free leaves that have just reached full size but are still tender. Wash and prepare, or refrigerate immediately.

Additional Information

Recommended kale varieties for Texas include 'Blue Knight', 'Dwarf Curled', 'Dwarf Scotch', 'Dwarf Siberian', 'Red Bor', and my favorite, 'Red Russian'. Though not necessarily bred to eat, the showy ornamental kales and cabbages are certainly edible. Kale originated in the Mediterranean.

LETTUCE

Producing nice heads of rather bland iceberg lettuce is difficult in Texas, but the many types and colors of leaf lettuce (*Lactuca sativa*) are fairly easy to grow, as long as they are provided with cool temperatures and adequate moisture. Starting with transplants instead of seed makes it much easier. Showy colored vegetables are higher in antioxidants, so be sure your salad has plenty of the red and burgundy forms of lettuce.

When to Plant

Lettuce is a cool-weather plant that blooms and dies when the weather is hot. Like many greens, the flavor gets bitter and the texture gets tougher with hot weather. Lettuce can tolerate frosts but not hard freezes, so it should be planted in late winter or early spring for an initial crop. A second fall crop can be planted around September in the northern half of Texas, and in October in the southern half of Texas. Lettuce can either be direct seeded or planted as transplants, which are often available from nurseries and garden centers. Transplants are much easier. The transplants should be planted 4 to 6 inches apart.

Where to Plant

Lettuce requires at least eight hours of direct sun each day, but like most leafy greens it can tolerate a bit of filtered light, or as little as five to six hours of direct sun. Just remember that any amount of shade reduces production. Plant lettuce in rich, well-drained soil, either in the ground or in containers at least 12 inches in diameter. Small containers dry out quickly in frequent warm temperatures. Ideally, till in several inches of organic matter and apply 2 pounds of a complete lawn or garden fertilizer (15-5-10, 13-13-13, and so forth) per 100 square feet of bed or every 35 feet of row. In small plots use 2 teaspoons per square foot or foot of row. The ideal soil pH for growing lettuce is 6.0 to 7.0.

How to Plant

Transplants should be planted in well-cultivated soil. Dig holes that are the same size as the existing pots they are growing in. Remove from the pots and place the roots into the freshly dug holes. Gently firm the soil around the transplants. Water them thoroughly with a water-soluble plant food at half the labeled recommendation.

Care and Maintenance

The keys to growing good lettuce are mild temperatures, high fertility, and regular moisture. Leaves that become old and tough will be bitter. Two weeks after transplanting, fertilize them with 1 cup of high-nitrogen fertilizer (21-0-0, and so forth) for each 35 feet of row. Sprinkle half of the fertilizer down each side of the row. Lightly work it into the soil and then water. After side dressing, apply a layer of organic mulch (hay, straw, grass clippings, and so forth) to conserve water and prevent weeds. Lettuce is relatively pest free, but be on the lookout for slugs, aphids, and assorted caterpillars.

Harvest

Depending on the variety, leaf lettuces are fully mature for harvesting the entire plant in forty to sixty-five days. However, any part of the plant is tender and edible from the time it germinates, so feel free to pick leaves to eat or to use entire plants that are thinned at any time. Either pick the large but still tender, pest-free, older leaves from the bottom of the plant, or cut the entire plant just above the ground. Wash and prepare, or refrigerate immediately.

Additional Information

Recommended lettuce varieties for Texas include 'Black Seeded Simpson' (leaf), 'Buttercrunch' (butterhead), 'Salad Bib' (butterhead), 'Green Ice' (leaf), 'Raisa' (leaf), 'Red Sails' (leaf), 'Red Salad Bowl' (leaf), 'Salad Bowl' (leaf), and 'Parris Island Cos' (romaine). Lettuce originated in Egypt or Iran.

MUSTARD GREENS

Cooked greens with ham hocks or salt pork and potliker (or potlikker) are eaten all over the South. Growing up in the Pineywoods of East Texas, I noticed that folks ate different greens according to geography and culture. My people here eat mostly turnip greens. But when I lived in southeast Texas, I noticed that most individuals preferred mustard greens (*Brassica juncea*). That's great news for a gardener because mustard greens have the largest leaves, and it takes less picking to fill a pot. The key to great mustard greens is to grow them in cool weather and harvest young tender leaves so they won't be bitter.

When to Plant

Mustard greens are cool-weather plants that bloom and die when the weather is hot. The greens' flavor gets stronger with heat as well. And like most greens, the texture gets tougher. Mustard greens can tolerate frosts but not hard freezes, so they should be planted in late winter or early spring for an initial crop. A second fall crop can be planted around September in the northern half of Texas, and in October in the southern half of Texas. Mustard is easily direct seeded into the garden. Once the seedlings are established and have true leaves, thin them to 4 to 6 inches apart.

Where to Plant

Mustard greens require at least eight hours of direct sun each day, but like most greens they can tolerate as little as five to six hours of direct sun. Just remember that any amount of shade reduces production. Plant mustard

greens in a rich, well-drained soil. Ideally, till in several inches of organic matter and apply 2 pounds of a complete lawn or garden fertilizer (15-5-10, 13-13-13, and so forth) per 100 square feet of bed or every 35 feet of row. In small plots use 2 teaspoons per square foot or foot of row. The ideal soil pH for growing mustard greens is 5.5 to 7.0.

How to Plant

Mustard greens can be grown either in beds or rows several feet apart. Scatter the seed on tilled soil that has been raked smooth. Gently rake the seed into the soil, making sure that it is no deeper than ¼ of an inch below the surface of the soil. Water gently and keep the soil moist until germination (sprouting) occurs. Then reduce the *frequency* of watering so that the plants gradually get tougher.

Care and Maintenance

The keys to growing good mustard greens are cool temperatures, high fertility, and frequent harvesting. Leaves that become old and tough will be bitter and hot tasting. To keep leaves fresh and tender, shear the entire plant with hedge clippers every two to three weeks and side-dress with a high-nitrogen fertilizer (21-0-0, and so forth) at 1 cup per 35 foot of row. Slugs as well as flea beetles can be a problem, especially during warm weather. Pick off the buggy leaves and treat the plants with an insecticide labeled for greens if necessary.

Harvest

Mustard greens are ready to harvest just thirty-five to fifty days after seeding. Any part of the plant is tender and edible from the time it germinates, so feel free to pick leaves to eat or to use entire plants that are thinned at any time. Either pick the large but still tender, pest-free older leaves from the bottom of the plant or cut the entire plant just above the ground. It's much better to pick mustard too soon rather than too late, as it will tend to get strongly flavored with age. Wash and prepare, or refrigerate immediately.

Additional Information

Recommended mustard green varieties for Texas include 'Florida Broadleaf', 'Green Wave', 'Southern Giant Curled', and 'Tendergreen'. Mustard greens are native to the Mediterranean.

OKRA

Introduced to the South with the slave trade, okra (*Abelmoschus esculentus*) is synonymous with Southern culture. It has been used as a thickening agent and table vegetable ever since. The African name for okra was gumbo and subsequently gave us the name for the popular Creole soup. I grew up with okra and like it raw, boiled, fried, and, of course, in gumbo.

When to Plant

Okra is a warm-season plant that cannot tolerate frosts or freezes. As a matter of fact, it can't even stand cool days or nights. It thrives on heat, so it should be planted well after the last frost in your region. This is generally March in the southern half of the state and April or later in the northern half of the state. Okra is easily planted from seed. Soak it in warm water overnight to speed up the germination (sprouting) process. Once the seedlings are established and about 6 inches tall, thin them to 12 to 18 inches apart. Occasionally okra transplants are available, which can be planted at the same spacing.

Where to Plant

Okra needs at least eight hours of direct sun each day for maximum production. It isn't picky about soils as long as they drain well. Due to a susceptibility to microscopic nematodes (parasitic worms), it is best to avoid areas where this has been a problem in the past or where okra was planted the previous year. Ideally, till in several inches of compost or organic matter and incorporate 2 pounds of a complete lawn or garden fertilizer (15-5-10, 13-13-13, and so forth) per 100 square feet of bed or every 35 feet of row before planting. For small plantings use 2 teaspoons per square foot or foot of row. The ideal soil pH for growing okra is 6.0 to 7.0.

How to Plant

Okra can be planted on flat ground or in raised beds or rows. The rows should be 6 to 8 inches high, 24 inches wide, and 36 to 48 inches apart. Using the corner of a hoe or a stick, open up a trench ½ to ¾ inch deep and plant the okra seed at a rate of four to five per foot of row. Cover the seed lightly with well-cultivated soil, and gently tamp down with the back of the hoe to conserve moisture and ensure good seed-to-soil contact.

Care and Maintenance

Okra is easy to grow and relatively pest free; however, a few potential problems include nematodes, cotton root rot, and fire ants. Cotton root rot can be a devastating problem, causing sudden death of the plants.

It has no cure. Discard the dead plants and try growing in a different area of your garden. Fire ants are the most common pest and can inflict damage to the blooms, young pods, and your hands. Treat the plants and the mounds with an appropriately labeled pesticide for okra and ants when they occur. After thinning, side-dress them with a high-nitrogen fertilizer.

Harvest

Okra is generally ready for harvesting about seventy days after planting the seed. Okra pods should be harvested when they are 3 to 5 inches long and tender. Sometimes they will snap from the plant, but I usually use a pair of hand pruners. Okra foliage irritates some gardeners' skin, so you might want to wear a long-sleeved shirt. Okra needs to be harvested every two to three days to keep producing well. If the pods are left on the plant until they get tough and the seeds plump up, the entire plant will stop producing.

Additional Information

Recommended okra varieties for Texas include 'Annie Oakley', 'Burgundy' (my favorite), 'Cajun Delight', 'Clemson Spineless', 'Emerald', and 'Lee'. 'Burgundy' okra turns green when you cook or pickle it. Okra is native to Africa.

ONION

Texans love their onions (*Allium cepa*), some even more than others. My dad grew up drinking his milk out of straws made with onion leaves and eats a big hunk of raw onion with every meal. Of course we are home to the 'Texas 1015Y' (Texas SuperSweet) onion, the "sweetest onion in the world." It's even our state vegetable. Onions are easy to grow if you remember to grow them when the temperatures are cool and the days are short.

When to Plant

Onions are cool-weather plants that bolt or bloom when the weather is hot and the days are long. For onion tops to be vigorous, tender, and mild, the weather must be cool. Onions can tolerate frosts but not hard freezes, so they should be planted from bundled bare-root transplants known as sets in late winter or early spring. To make large onion bulbs, it's very important to plant them as early as possible. Late-planted onions produce small bulbs.

Where to Plant

Onions require at least eight hours of direct sun each day for maximum yields. Like most root crops, they do best in well-drained sandy and loamy soils, and they are best planted in raised beds or rows at least 6 to 12 inches high. Ideally, till in several inches of compost or organic matter, and incorporate 2 pounds of a complete lawn or garden fertilizer (15-5-10, 13-13-13, and so forth) per 100 square feet of bed or every 35 feet of row before planting. In smaller plantings use 2 teaspoons of fertilizer per square foot or foot of row. The ideal soil pH for growing onions is 5.5 to 7.0.

How to Plant

Onions can be grown in raised beds or raised rows 6 inches high, 18 inches wide, and 36 inches apart. Use a stick or hoe handle to poke holes into the soil 1 inch deep. Place the transplants, root side down, into each hole. Gently firm them in, and water immediately to settle the soil around them.

Care and Maintenance

Onions are relatively easy to grow, provided they have lots of sunshine, cool temperatures, and regular moisture when bulbing. Around three to four weeks after planting or when the plants are 6 inches tall, fertilize them with 1 cup of high-nitrogen fertilizer (21-0-0, and so forth) for each 35 feet of row. Sprinkle half of the fertilizer down each side of the row. Lightly work it into the soil and then water. When cultivating, be careful not to damage the base of the plant. Hand weeding around the plants is best. After side-dressing with fertilizer, apply a layer of organic mulch (hay, straw, grass clippings, and so forth) to conserve water and prevent weeds. Despite what old-timers may have told you, the more foliage your onions make, the larger the bulbs will be when the days start to get longer and the bulbs begin to form. Every leaf forms a ring in the onion.

Harvest

Green onions can be harvested at any time during the life of the onion. They, of course, are most tender when they are small. Onion bulbs are ready to harvest when the necks of the plants get soft and the tops fall over. They should be pulled or dug at this point and allowed to cure for several days in a cool, dry area. The tops should then be cut off 1 inch above the onion. This curing process helps them store longer.

Additional Information

Recommended varieties for Texas include 'Texas 1015Y' (Texas Supersweet), 'Grano 502', 'Granex', 'Granex 33', 'White Granex', 'Red Granex', and 'Burgundy'. Various strains of perennial multiplying onions are grown for green onions during the winter and spring. They are planted in the fall then dug and divided when dormant during the summer. Onions are native to Pakistan.

OREGANO

Italian cooking wouldn't be the same without oregano (*Origanum vulgare*). I can't even imagine the flavor of spaghetti, lasagna, or pizza without it. Oregano is easy to grow as long as your start with a nursery-grown transplant and provide it with well-drained soil and full sun. I generally grow it in a large container so I can trim the shoots that drape over the side.

When to Plant

Oregano is planted from transplants after all danger of frost in the spring. It tolerates frosts and light freezes and thrives with mild and moderately warm temperatures. If summer heat and drought kill your initial planting, another crop can be planted in early autumn. Although a single plant generally produces enough for a small family, an 18- to 24-inch spacing is generally sufficient for multiple plants.

Where to Plant

Like most Mediterranean herbs, oregano requires at least eight hours of direct sun each day. It should be planted in a well-drained soil, either in the ground or in containers at least 12 inches in diameter or preferably larger. Small containers dry out quickly in Texas's frequent warm temperatures, leading to plant death or stress. Ideally, till several inches of organic matter into the soil and incorporate 2 pounds of a complete lawn or garden fertilizer (15-5-10, 13-13-13, and so forth) per 100 square feet of bed or every 35 feet of row. In small plots use 2 teaspoons per square foot or foot of row. The ideal soil pH for growing oregano is 6.0 to 7.0.

How to Plant

Oregano can be grown either in the ground or containers. Use large containers, as the oregano benefits from the additional drainage provided. Add 2 teaspoons of slow-release fertilizer into the soil for each plant. Transplants should be planted into a professional-grade, well-drained potting soil. Dig a hole that is the same size as the existing pot the oregano is growing in. Gently firm the soil around it, being careful not to plant the transplant any deeper than it was growing in the pot. Water thoroughly with a water-soluble plant food such as Miracle-Gro at half the labeled recommendation. If planting in the ground, consider placing several pieces of brick or concrete rubble on the prepared soil, placing the oregano on top of it, and filling in around it with professional-grade potting soil and perhaps a gravel or decomposed granite mulch. This mound planting improves the drainage and more closely mimics oregano's Mediterranean habitat.

Care and Maintenance

Oregano is easy to grow and relatively pest free. To stimulate new tender foliage, keep it trimmed or harvested regularly and apply a water-soluble fertilizer every one to two weeks. In heavy clay soils, oregano may have a tendency to rot during wet weather.

Harvest

Tender shoots and oregano leaves can be harvested at any time within weeks of transplanting. I find harvesting with a pair of scissors easiest. The more you cut the plant, the more it will make tender shoots and leaves. Discard any woody stems, and use or refrigerate immediately. Oregano can also be dried for later use.

Additional Information

Recommended oregano types for Texas include Greek oregano and Spanish oregano. Oregano is native to Greece and Spain.

PARSLEY

Although most often associated as an herb or as a garnish, you'll want to eat as much parsley (*Petroselinum crispum*) as you can, as it's extremely nutritious. I used to frequent a restaurant in San Antonio that served it fried to a crisp and it was wonderful. Parsley can be frilly and curled or flat leafed, and it is easy to grow, as long as you start with a nursery-grown transplant. It must be grown when the temperatures are cool and moist.

When to Plant

Parsley is a cool-weather plant that bolts or goes to seed when the weather is hot. Its flavor gets stronger with heat as well. For parsley to be vigorous and tender, the weather must be cool. Parsley can tolerate frosts but not hard freezes, so it should be planted in late winter or early spring for an initial crop. A second fall crop can be planted around September in the northern half of Texas, and in October in the southern half of Texas. Parsley is planted from transplants, which are often available from nurseries and garden centers. They should be placed 12 inches apart.

Where to Plant

Parsley requires at least eight hours of direct sun each day but can tolerate a bit of filtered light, or as little as five to six hours of direct sun. It should be planted in a rich, well-drained soil, either in the ground or in containers at least 12 inches in diameter or preferably larger. Small containers dry out quickly in the frequent warm temperatures of Texas, leading to plant death or stress. Ideally, till several inches of organic matter into the soil and incorporate 2 pounds of a complete lawn or garden fertilizer (15-5-10, 13-13-13, and so forth) per 100 square feet of bed or every 35 feet of row. In small plots use 2 teaspoons per square foot or foot of row. The ideal pH for growing parsley is 6.0 to 7.0.

How to Plant

Parsley can be grown either in the ground or containers. I prefer the ground so the plants don't dry out as much. Transplants should be planted in well-cultivated soil. Dig holes that are the same size as the existing pot the parsley is growing in. Gently firm the soil around the transplant, being careful not to plant it any deeper than it was growing in the pot. Water thoroughly with a water-soluble plant food at half the labeled recommendation.

Care and Maintenance

Parsley is relatively easy to grow. To promote new shoots and foliage, pick leaves and remove flowers regularly, and apply several teaspoons of a lawn

and garden fertilizer (15-5-10, 13-13-13, and so forth) every two to three weeks or a water-soluble fertilizer every one to two weeks. The main pest to look out for is the larva (caterpillar) of the beautiful eastern black swallowtail butterfly. Many gardeners leave them alone and plant extra parsley for the butterflies.

Harvest

The fully expanded but still tender lower leaves of parsley can be harvested at any time within weeks of transplanting. Pull pest-free leaves from the base of the plant, and wash, use, or refrigerate immediately. Parsley leaves can also be dried and stored for later use.

Additional Information

Recommended varieties for Texas include 'Moss Curled', 'Petra', 'Triple Curled', and 'Italian Flat Leaf'. Parsley is native to the Mediterranean.

POTATO

When I was a small boy, the elderly Mr. Adams, who lived through the woods and up the hill from our house, asked me to help him plant his potato (*Solanum tuberosum*) crop. I remember how intrigued I was at putting pieces of potatoes into the soft loamy soil. The day we pulled them up and scratched out multitudes of large whole potatoes was the day I became a vegetable gardener. It was truly magic. He sent me home with a heavy grocery sack full of them, and my mom prepared them for me the way she ate them as a little girl. I was hooked.

When to Plant

Potatoes are cool-weather plants that bloom and die when the temperatures get hot. They can tolerate frosts but not hard freezes and are mostly planted as a spring crop in Texas. They should be planted about four weeks before the last expected frost. For many in the state, Valentine's Day is potato planting day. Potatoes are planted from small potatoes or pieces of larger potatoes known as seed potatoes. They should be spaced 8 to 12 inches apart.

Where to Plant

Potatoes require at least eight hours of direct sun each day for maximum yields. Like most root crops, they do best in well-drained sandy and loamy soils and are best planted in raised beds or rows at least 6 to 12 inches high. Ideally, till in several inches of compost or organic matter and incorporate

2 pounds of a complete lawn or garden fertilizer (15–5–10, 13–13–13, and so forth) per 100 square feet of bed or every 35 feet of row before planting. In smaller plantings use 2 teaspoons per square foot or foot of row. The ideal soil pH for growing potatoes is 5.0 to 6.5.

How to Plant

Potatoes can be grown in raised beds or raised rows 6 inches high, 18 inches wide, and 36 inches apart. Use your hoe to open up a furrow 3 inches deep down in the row. Place the seed pieces or small potatoes in the bottom of the furrow. Cover them with well-cultivated soil and gently firm them in with the back of your hoe.

Care and Maintenance

Potatoes are relatively easy to grow, provided they have lots of sunshine and cool temperatures. Around three to four weeks after planting or when the plants are 6 inches tall, use your hoe or shovel to apply about 3 to 4 inches of dirt or compost to the bases of the plants. This creates a desirable area for the potatoes to form in. Ideally, apply a layer of organic mulch (hay, straw, grass clippings, and so forth) to conserve water and prevent weeds. The main pest on potatoes is the potato bug that eats the foliage. Handpick them or apply an appropriately labeled pesticide.

Harvest

Potatoes are usually ready to harvest 90 to 120 days after planting. Spring-planted plants indicate when they are ready to harvest as the tops turn yellow and start to die. I usually start sneaking some tender new potatoes as soon as the plants start blooming by gently probing beneath them with my fingers. Be careful not to disturb the root system, and always remember your production will be greater if you leave them alone until they are mature. I can't help myself though. If you are going to consume the final crop rather quickly, dig them with a spading fork and wash them before storing in a cool, humid, dark place. If you want to store them for a longer period of time, cut the tops off the dying plants and leave the potatoes in the ground for three to four days. This will toughen the skins and make the potatoes last longer.

Additional Information

Recommended potato varieties for Texas include 'Kennebec' (white), 'Pontiac' (red), 'Red Lasoda' (red), and 'Norland' (red). Potatoes are native to South America.

PUMPKIN

What child among us, or in us, doesn't like picking out a pumpkin (*Cucurbita pepo*)? And what baby boomer didn't grow up hoping Linus would finally see the Great Pumpkin? And who doesn't wish they could grow their very own? It's not easy in Texas, but it can be done. The key is planting during the late summer and providing water until fall arrives. There are a number of obstacles in your way, including powdery mildew, viruses, and squash vine borers. You can do it though. Linus and I both have faith.

When to Plant

Pumpkins require warm soils to germinate. If a summer crop is wanted, they should be planted in the spring after all danger of frost has passed (generally April in the northern half of Texas and March in the southern half). They cannot tolerate frost or freezes. To produce a fall crop of jack-o'-lanterns, plant the seed approximately four months (generally around July) before the first killing frost in your area. Different varieties have different number of days to reach maturity, so be sure to check the variety description and add about 25 days for slower maturity in the fall. Nobody said it was easy! Pumpkins should be planted in hills 4 to 6 feet apart and thinned to the strongest two plants seven to ten days after sprouting.

Where to Plant

Pumpkins require at least eight hours of direct sun each day for maximum production. They aren't choosy about soils as long as the soil drains well. Ideally, till in several inches of compost or organic matter and incorporate 2 pounds of a complete lawn or garden fertilizer (15-5-10, 13-13-13, and so forth) per 100 square feet of bed or every 35 feet of row before planting. The ideal soil pH for growing pumpkins is 6.0 to 7.5.

How to Plant

Pumpkins are direct seeded into the garden and make very large plants. Create a raised row about 6 inches high and 12 inches wide. Multiple rows should be around 8 feet apart. Pumpkin seed should be planted in groups of seed every 6 feet. This is known as planting in hills. Open a shallow depression about 1 inch deep and 4 inches wide with a hoe. Drop four to five seeds evenly spaced apart in the hole and cover lightly with loose soil using a hoe or garden rake.

Care and Maintenance

About three weeks after thinning your pumpkins, apply an additional application of fertilizer. This is known as sidedressing. Sprinkle 2 tablespoons of a high-nitrogen fertilizer (21-0-0, and so forth) around each hill, being careful to keep it off the plants. Work the fertilizer into the soil lightly with a hoe or rake and water. After side-dressing, it is ideal to apply a layer of organic mulch (hay, straw, grass clippings, and so forth) to conserve water and prevent weeds. The most common pest problems on pumpkins are cucumber beetles, squash bugs, vine borers, powdery mildew, and viruses. Control the insects as they occur with appropriately labeled insecticides. There is no cure for a virus, but controlling the cucumber beetles will help lessen its occurrence.

Harvest

Pumpkins should be ready to harvest 90 to 120 days after planting the seed, depending on the variety. The pumpkins are ripe when they are fully colored and have a hard rind and a woody stem. Cut the pumpkin from the plant with a pair of hand pruners leaving a 3- to 4-inch stem on the fruit. Fall pumpkins can tolerate frosts without damaging the fruit but should be harvested and protected if the temperatures are going to dip below 30 degrees.

Additional Information

Recommended pumpkin varieties in Texas include 'Big Max', 'Connecticut Field', 'Funny Face', 'Jack-B-Little', 'Jack O'Lantern', 'Jackpot', 'Small Sugar', and 'Spirit Hybrid'. Pumpkins are native to Central and South America.

RADISH

Radishes (*Raphanus sativus*) are so easy to grow that they are among the first vegetables included in children's gardens. Unfortunately, very few children eat radishes! Their spicy bite is more of an acquired taste for adults. Of course, they make colorful garnishes for plates and salads alike. All you need is friable (loose) soil and the cool temperatures of fall, mild winter, and early spring.

When to Plant

Radishes are cool-weather plants that bolt or go to seed when the weather is hot. Their flavor gets stronger and hotter with heat as well. The roots can get tough and pithy with the onset of hot weather. Radishes can tolerate frosts but not hard freezes, so they should be planted in late winter or early spring for an initial crop. A second fall crop can be planted around September in the northern half of Texas and in October in the southern half of Texas. Radishes are easily direct seeded into the garden. Once the seedlings are established and have their first true leaves, thin them to 1 to 2 inches apart.

Where to Plant

Radishes require at least eight hours of direct sun each day for maximum yields. Like most root crops, they do best in well-drained sandy and loamy soils and are best planted in raised beds or rows at least 6 to 12 inches high.

Ideally, till in several inches of compost or organic matter and incorporate 1 pound of a complete lawn or garden fertilizer (15-5-10, 13-13-13, and so forth) per 100 square feet of bed or every 35 feet of row before planting. In smaller plantings use 1 teaspoon per square foot or foot of row. The ideal soil pH for growing radishes is 6.0 to 7.0.

How to Plant

Radishes can be grown either in beds or rows 2 to 3 feet apart. Open a shallow trench in your raised row ½ inch deep with the corner of a hoe or a stick. Sow the seeds three to four per inch to ensure a good stand, and cover with ¼ to ½ inch of soil. Another option is to sprinkle the seeds on top of the row or bed and lightly rake the surface to cover them. After seeding, gently tamp down the soil with the back of your hoe to ensure good seed-to-soil contact. Water gently and keep the soil moist until germination occurs. When the seedlings are up, reduce the *frequency* of watering so that the plants gradually get hardier. In order for radishes to form properly, it's critical that the seedlings be thinned within two to three days of sprouting.

Care and Maintenance

Radishes are extremely easy to grow. They produce so quickly there's generally no need (or time) for an additional application of fertilizer. A layer of organic mulch (straw, hay, and so forth) around them is ideal. They have very few pest problems.

Harvest

Radishes are generally ready to harvest within twenty to thirty days after planting. Harvest radishes when they are small and tender, approximately 1 inch in diameter. Large radishes get tough, hot, and spicy. Pull and discard them. Wash and serve, or refrigerate the tender ones immediately.

Additional Information

Recommended radish varieties for Texas include 'Champion', 'Cherry Belle', 'Red Prince', 'Sparkler', and 'White Icicle'. Radishes originated in China.

ROSEMARY

Okay, rosemary (*Rosmarinus officinalis*) isn't a fruit or a vegetable, so get over it. It grows well in Texas and goes well with lots of things that we do eat, including most meats and potatoes. It's also pretty, historic, and a long-time symbol of remembrance. All you need is full sun and excellent drainage to grow it. So see if you can't remember to plant some.

When to Plant

Rosemary is planted from transplants after all danger of frost in the spring has passed. It tolerates frosts and light freezes and thrives with warm temperatures. In much of Texas, it's a cold-hardy perennial. Although a single plant is generally enough for a small family, 24-inch spacing is generally sufficient for multiple plants.

Where to Plant

Like many Mediterranean herbs, rosemary requires at least eight hours of direct sun each day. Anything less and your rosemary will be weak and spindly. Plant rosemary in any well-drained soil, either in the ground or in containers at least 12 inches in diameter or preferably larger. Small containers dry out quickly in Texas's frequent warm temperatures, leading to plant death or stress. In humid, high-rainfall areas, it's a good idea to plant rosemary in a raised bed. The ideal pH for growing rosemary is 6.0 to 7.0, although it's known for being quite alkaline (high pH) tolerant.

How to Plant

If using a container, the transplant should be planted into professional-grade, well-drained potting soil. Dig a hole that is the same size as the existing pot that the plant is growing in. Gently firm the soil around it, being careful not to plant the transplant any deeper than it was growing in the pot. Water thoroughly with a water-soluble plant food such as Miracle-Gro at half the labeled recommendation. If planting in the ground, consider placing some broken brick or concrete rubble on top of the ground, planting the rosemary on top of it, and pulling the dirt up around the rubble and rosemary roots, creating a raised, well-drained mound. Adding a gravel or decomposed granite mulch is even better. This improved drainage more mimics rosemary's Mediterranean habitat and ensures survival during periods of heavy rainfall.

Care and Maintenance

Rosemary is easy to grow and relatively pest free. To stimulate new tender foliage, keep it trimmed or harvested regularly. Rosemary is a light feeder

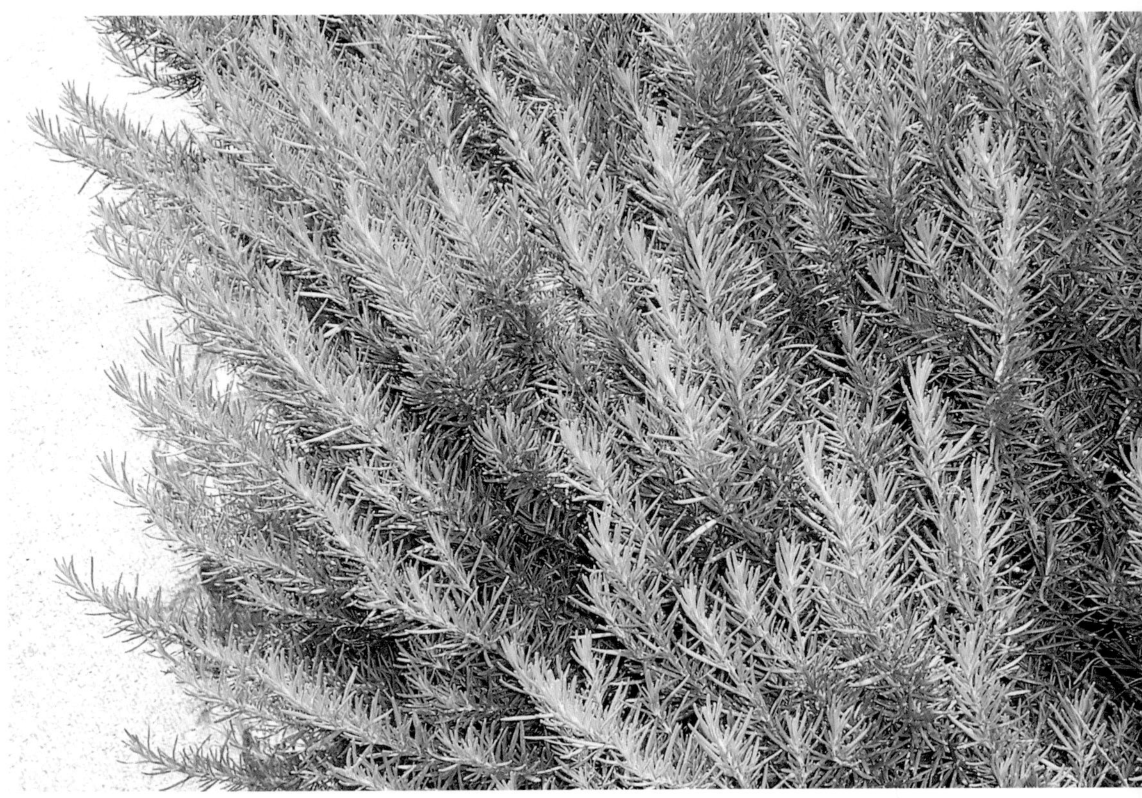

and only needs a sprinkle of lawn or garden fertilizer each spring. In heavy clay soils, rosemary may have a tendency to rot during wet weather. After winter, trim out any dead branches.

Harvest

Tender rosemary shoots and leaves can be harvested at any time within weeks of transplanting. I find harvesting with a pair of scissors easiest. The more you cut the plant, the more tender shoots and leaves it will make. Use or refrigerate immediately. Although most folks discard the woody stems, some use them as skewers for added flavor when grilling kebabs or other foods.

Additional Information

Recommended rosemary varieties for Texas include 'Albus', 'Arp', 'Bendenen Blue', 'Collingwood Ingram', 'Corsicus' (Corsican), 'Erectus', 'Majorca', 'Prostratus', 'Roman Vivace', and 'Tuscan Blue'. Rosemary is native to the Mediterranean and produces blue, pink, or white flowers during the winter.

SHELL BEAN

My top three favorite traditional vegetables consumed fresh from the garden are new potatoes, sweet corn, and fresh pinto beans (*Phaseolus* spp.). When it comes to dried beans from the store versus fresh-shelled ones from the garden, there's no comparison. Whether pinto, butter, or lima, eat up. They are high in protein as well as fiber. They literally combine meat and vegetable into one dish. As an added bonus, they enrich the soil with the nitrogen they produce on their roots.

When to Plant

Beans require warm soils to germinate and should be planted after all danger of frost in the spring (generally April in the northern half of Texas and March in the southern half). Planting too soon will result in poor germination and stunted plants. However, if you wait too long after the last frost, you will most likely have to deal with dry conditions and a poor harvest. A fall crop of shell beans can be planted at least three to four months before the first killing frost. Just remember that shell beans mature best when the temperatures are in the 70s. After the young plants establish themselves and have their first true leaves, thin them to 4 to 6 inches apart.

Where to Plant

Shell beans require at least eight hours of direct sun each day. Beans aren't terribly picky about soil types but should be planted in areas that drain well. Ideally, till in several inches of compost or organic matter into the soil if possible, and incorporate 2 pounds of a complete garden fertilizer (13-13-13, 10-20-10, and so forth) per 100 square feet of bed or every 35 feet of row. The ideal soil pH for growing shell beans is 5.8 to 7.0.

How to Plant

Beans are direct seeded into the garden. Create a raised row about 6 inches high and 8 to 12 inches wide. Multiple rows should be around 36 inches apart. Open a shallow trench 1 to 1 ½ inches deep with the corner of a hoe or a stick. Drop the seed several inches apart to ensure a good stand. Cover lightly with loose soil using a hoe or garden rake. If the seed is too deep, it won't germinate.

Care and Maintenance

Check the progress of your bean plants when they are 6 to 8 inches tall. If they are vigorous and healthy, you don't need to do a thing. If they are pale green and not vigorous, you will need to apply a high-nitrogen fertilizer to stimulate their growth. Use 1 cup of ammonium sulfate (21-0-0) for every 35 feet of row. Sprinkle half of the fertilizer down each side of the row. Lightly work it into the soil and then water. This extra fertilizer application to boost the plants along is known as sidedressing. Beans are relatively pest free; however, watch for aphids, stinkbugs, spider mites, and rust. Treat with a safe, labeled pesticide if needed.

Harvest

Bush-type shell beans are generally ready to pick in sixty-five to seventy-five days. Pole-type shell beans generally take seventy-five to eight-five days. Pick fresh beans when the pods become yellowish (or reddish, depending on the variety) and the beans are plump inside. The beans should pop out easily when you press on the pod seam with your thumb. Dry shell beans are left on the plant until fully dried and either harvested one pod at a time or by pulling or cutting the entire plant and thrashing the seed loose.

Additional Information

Recommended varieties for Texas include 'Dwarf Horticultural' (improved pinto), 'Dixie Speckled Butterpea' (butterbean), 'Dixie White Butterpea' (butterbean), 'Henderson Bush' (baby lima), 'Thorogreen' (baby lima), 'Jackson Wonder' (speckled lima), 'Florida Speckled' (speckled lima), 'Christmas-Pole' (speckled lima), and 'Sieva-Pole' (baby Lima). Shell beans originated in Central America.

SNOW PEA

We all have a veggie garden wish list—things we wish we could grow but aren't or can't. One of the delicacies that often tops that list is the snow pea (*Pisum sativum*). Fresh snow peas from the garden are so delicate and crisp that the immediate tendency is to scarf them all up before reaching the kitchen. Like English peas, snow peas can't take severe cold or much heat. That doesn't leave much else. I have the best experience planting in the fall, and will do whatever it takes even for a small crop.

When to Plant

Snow peas are cool-weather plants that die when the weather is hot. They can tolerate frosts but not hard freezes and are best adapted as a fall crop in Texas, planted eight to ten weeks before the first freeze is expected. Growing snow peas as a spring crop in Texas is very difficult due to our fast-warming temperatures. In mild, southern areas of the state, they can be planted in midwinter for a risky spring harvest. Snow peas are almost always direct seeded into the garden. When the young peas have been up for about a week, the dwarf types should be thinned to 2 to 3 inches apart and the climbing types to 5 inches apart.

Where to Plant

Snow peas require at least eight hours of direct sun each day. They aren't terribly picky about soil types but should be planted in areas that drain well. Ideally, till several inches of compost or organic matter into the soil if possible and incorporate 1 pound of a complete garden fertilizer (13-13-13, 10-20-10, and so forth) per 100 square foot of bed or every 35 feet of row. In smaller areas use 1 teaspoon per square feet or foot of row. The ideal soil pH for growing snow peas is 5.8 to 7.0.

How to Plant

It is generally recommended that snow peas be direct seeded into the garden. Create a raised row about 6 inches high and 16 to 24 inches wide. Multiple rows should be around 30 to 48 inches apart. Open a shallow trench 1 to 1½ inches deep with the corner of a hoe or a stick. Drop the seed several inches apart to ensure a good stand. Cover lightly with loose soil using a hoe or garden rake.

Care and Maintenance

It is important to keep your snow peas watered regularly. When the soil is dry 1 inch below the surface, water until it's wet to a depth of 6 to 8 inches. Applying an organic mulch of compost, straw, or grass clippings will help conserve moisture, stabilize the soil temperature, and prevent weeds. Avoid excessive fertilization, which will lead to unnecessary foliage growth and delayed flowering. All true peas have a desire to climb. The dwarf types will twine upon themselves; however, the climbing types will need cattle panels, chicken wire, concrete reinforcing wire, or snow (pea) fencing to climb on. Luckily, insects and diseases are not a major problem. Heat, drought, and excessive cold are, however.

Harvest

Snow peas are ready to harvest around seventy days after planting. Snow peas are edible and can be picked when they are very small, but they have their best flavor when the pods are full sized yet still tender with the peas inside the size of BBs. Hold the vine just below the pod with one hand and pull the pod with the other to avoid damaging the vine. Harvest snow peas just before eating or cooking for the best flavor.

Additional Information

Recommended snow pea varieties for Texas include 'Dwarf Gray Sugar', 'Mammoth Melting Sugar', and 'Oregon Sugar Pod II'. Snow peas are native to Asia.

SOUTHERN PEA

When you say the word *pea* to most gardeners in the world, they think of green English or snap peas that thrive in cool, moist environments. But to most Texans and Southerners, a hot-weather legume from Africa, more related to beans, is the norm. Despite what Northerners say about our peas (*Vigna unguiculata*) being cattle food, many of our ancestors dined on them practically daily throughout their lives. They are easy to grow, very productive, and very nutritious. Southern peas come in many varieties and colors, including both standard types and those fat ones crowded into their pods known as crowders. I never met any Southern pea I didn't like. You can get black-eyed peas dried or canned, but no pea holds a candle to fresh ones from your own garden.

When to Plant

Southern peas are a warm-season crop that cannot tolerate frosts or freezes. As a matter of fact, they can't even stand cool days or nights. They thrive on heat, so they should be planted well after the last frost in your region. This is generally March in the southern half of the state and April or later in the northern half of the state. Southern peas are easily planted from seed. Once the seedlings are established and about 3 to 4 inches tall, thin them to 6 to 8 inches apart.

Where to Plant

Southern peas require at least eight hours of direct sun each day. They aren't terribly picky about soil types but should be planted in areas that drain well. Ideally, till several inches of compost or organic matter into the soil if possible and incorporate 1 pound of a complete garden fertilizer (13-13-13, 10-20-10, and so forth) per 100 square feet of bed or every 35 feet of row. The ideal soil pH for growing Southern peas is 6.0 to 7.0.

How to Plant

Create a raised row about 4 to 6 inches high and 16 to 24 inches wide. Multiple rows should be around 36 inches apart. Open a shallow trench 1½ inches deep with the corner of a hoe or a stick. Drop the seeds several inches apart to ensure a good stand. Cover lightly with loose soil using a hoe or garden rake.

Care and Maintenance

Southern peas are easy to grow and fairly drought tolerant. My most frequent problem growing them is with aphids, which can be controlled with an appropriately labeled insecticide.

Harvest

Depending on the variety, Southern peas are generally ready to pick seventy to ninety days from planting the seed. Pick fresh peas when the pods become yellowish, reddish, or purple, depending on the variety and when the peas are plump inside. Be sure to pick them before they turn brown and dry out. The peas should pop out easily when you press on the pod seam with your thumb. Peas picked too green are much more difficult, if not impossible, to shell. Small, thin, undeveloped peas are sometimes picked and cooked as "snaps" with the shelled peas.

Additional Information

Recommended Southern pea varieties for Texas include 'Black Crowder' (crowder), 'California #5' (black-eyed), 'Cream #40' (cream), 'Mississippi Silver Skin' (crowder), 'Pink Eye Purple Hull' (purple hull), and 'Zipper Cream' (cream, crowder). Southern peas are often eaten on New Year's Day throughout the South for good luck throughout the coming year. Cow peas, field peas, black-eyed peas, and crowder peas are all different names referring to Southern peas, which are native to Africa.

SPINACH

Most kids my age grew up loving Popeye and hating spinach. It usually came from a can and was slimy and bland. Of course fresh spinach (*Spinacea oleracea*) from your own garden tastes much different. It can be lightly cooked or, even better, eaten fresh. It's very tasty and much better for you than lettuce. It's a cool-season crop, so make sure to grow it in the fall, mild winters, and early spring.

When to Plant

Spinach is a cool-weather plant that dies when the weather is hot. Like most greens, the texture gets tougher with hot weather. Spinach can tolerate frosts but not hard freezes, so it should be planted in late winter or early spring for an initial crop. A second fall crop can be planted around September in the northern half of Texas and in October in the southern half of Texas. Spinach can either be direct seeded or planted as transplants, which are often available from garden centers. Once the seedlings are established and have their first true leaves, thin them to (or plant the transplants) 4 to 6 inches apart.

Where to Plant

Spinach requires at least eight hours of direct sun each day but can tolerate a bit of filtered light, or as little as five to six hours of direct sun. Plant spinach in a rich, well-drained soil, either in the ground or in containers at least 12 inches in diameter. Ideally, till several inches of organic matter into the soil and apply 1 pound of a complete lawn and garden fertilizer (15-5-10, 13-13-13, and so forth) per 100 square feet of bed or every 35 feet of row. In small plots use 1 teaspoon per square foot or foot of row. The ideal pH for growing spinach is 6.0 to 7.0.

How to Plant

Spinach can be grown either in beds or rows 2 to 3 feet apart. To improve seedling germination (sprouting), soak spinach seed in water for one to two days in the refrigerator. Open a shallow trench in your raised row ½ inch deep with the corner of a hoe or a stick. Drop the seed at a rate of 8 to 10 per foot of row to ensure a good stand. Water gently and keep the soil moist until germination occurs. When the seedlings are up, reduce the *frequency* of watering so that the plants gradually toughen up. Transplants should be planted in well-cultivated soil in holes dug the same size as the existing pots. Water them thoroughly with a water-soluble plant food at half the labeled recommendation.

Care and Maintenance

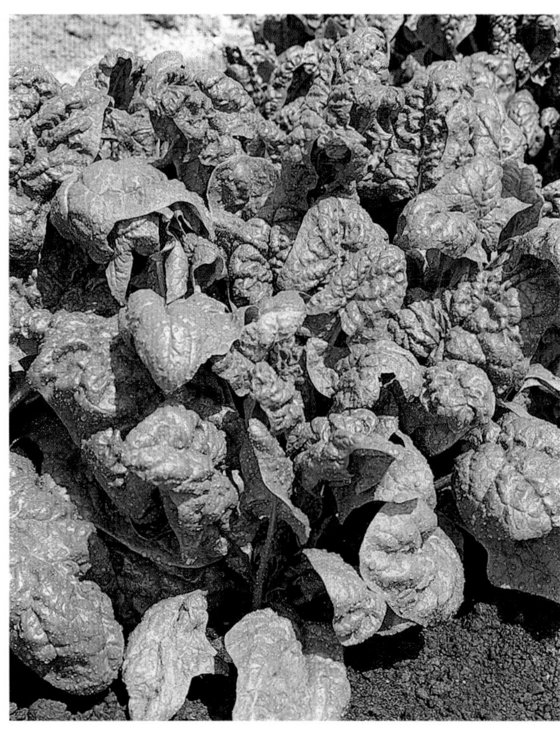

The keys to growing spinach are mild temperatures and regular moisture. Two weeks after thinning or transplanting, fertilize spinach with ½ cup of high-nitrogen fertilizer (21-0-0, and so forth) for each 35 feet of row. Sprinkle half of the fertilizer down each side of the row. Lightly work it into the soil and then water. After side-dressing with fertilizer, apply a layer of organic mulch (hay, straw, grass clippings, and so forth) to conserve water and prevent weeds. Others critters like spinach too, so be on the lookout for aphids and assorted caterpillars.

Harvest

Depending on the variety and the weather, spinach is generally ready to harvest within seven to ten weeks from seeding or much less from transplants. Harvest the older, pest-free leaves one leaf at a time, or cut the entire plant at the base and use all the leaves. Pick and cut often to stimulate new, tender leaves. Wash and prepare, or refrigerate immediately.

Additional Information

Recommended spinach varieties for Texas include 'America', 'Bloomsdale Longstanding', 'Coho', 'Dixie Market', 'Fall Green', 'Green Valley II', 'Hybrid 7', 'Iron Duke', 'Melody', 'Ozarka II', and 'Samish'. Spinach originated in Iran.

SUGAR CANE

Before granulated sugar became available in rural Texas and the South, most families grew sugar cane (*Sacchardum officinarum*) for making ribbon cane syrup. In addition to being used as a daily breakfast syrup on biscuits, it was used as a sugar substitute throughout the year for making pies, cakes, cookies, and candies. Youngsters prized the stalks themselves for chewing and extracting out the sweet sap. I grow heirloom sugar cane for syrup-making on the same property my great-grandparents, Jake and Dee Smith, had a syrup mill. It's a sweet but intensive labor of love.

When to Plant

Sugar cane is planted from stalks of "seed cane" in the spring after all danger of frost has passed in the northern half of Texas, and in the spring or fall in the southern half of Texas. It's a warm-season tropical perennial grass and can't tolerate frosts or freezes. Ideally, the cane sprouts at every node (joint), which potentially provides a plant every 1 to 2 feet. I generally aim for at least one plant every 36 inches.

Where to Plant

Sugar cane requires at least eight hours of direct sun each day for maximum yields. It performs best in moist, loamy soils. Traditionally, it was planted in

creek and river bottoms where the soil stayed moist through the summer. Ideally, till in several inches of compost or organic matter and incorporate 2 pounds of a complete lawn or garden fertilizer (15-5-10, 13-13-13, and so forth) per 100 square feet of bed or every 35 feet of row before planting. The ideal soil pH for growing sugar cane is 6.0 to 7.0.

How to Plant

Prepare raised rows 8 to 12 inches high. Open up a trench 6 inches deep down the middle of the row. Lay stalks of stripped seed cane in the trench, end to end, and cover with well-cultivated soil. If the stalks are old or damaged, overlap by half.

Care and Maintenance

Like corn, sugar cane is a grass and fairly easy to grow if you follow the basic rules of growing grass. It requires regular moisture of about 1 inch of water per week. It's also important to apply additional high-nitrogen fertilizer (21-0-0, and so forth) several times during the growth of the plant for maximum production. When the plants are about waist high, fertilize them with 1 cup of high-nitrogen fertilizer (21-0-0, and so forth) for each 35 feet of row. Sprinkle half of the fertilizer down each side of the row. Lightly work it into the soil and then water. When the plants reach head high, apply the same fertilizer at the same rate. The old-timers always used cottonseed meal for their sugar cane fertilizer.

Harvest

Sugar cane takes a full growing season, from last frost to first frost, to mature. Being a tropical grass, it can't take freezing temperatures, so be sure to harvest it before the first hard freeze. The longer it grows, the sweeter it gets, especially as the days get shorter and cooler. In my area, I normally try to harvest it a week before Thanksgiving unless there's an earlier freeze. Sugar cane is harvested by hand, by cutting it at the ground with a large cane knife or machete. Pruning loppers may also be used. The foliage is then stripped from the stalk using the same cane knife. Store it in a cool, moist place until ready to use or process.

Additional Information

Recommended sugar cane varieties for Texas include 'Louisiana Blue Ribbon Cane' and 'POJ' varieties. Other heirloom strains are often passed around, which also do well. It takes 8 to 10 gallons of raw sugar cane juice to make 1 gallon of cooked syrup. Sugar cane originated in Asia.

SUMMER SQUASH

I've been growing yellow squash (*Cucurbita pepo melopepo*) all my life because it's my momma's favorite vegetable. One year she told me she could eat her weight in squash so I planted an entire row for her. You should have heard her squeal when I showed up with 300 pounds of yellow squash! I was just guessing. If you slice straightneck squash long ways, then batter it and fry it, it makes a good veggie fish substitute. Put a little cocktail sauce on it and the kids may not know the difference.

When to Plant

Summer squash requires warm soil to germinate and should be planted in the spring after all danger of frost has passed (generally April in the northern half of Texas and March in the southern half). It cannot tolerate frost or freezes. A fall crop of summer squash can be planted about four months before the first killing frost. Squash is easily direct seeded into the garden. Once the seedlings are established and have their first true leaves, thin them to 24 to 30 inches apart.

Where to Plant

Summer squash requires at least eight hours of direct sun each day for maximum production. It isn't picky about soils as long as they drain well. Ideally, till in several inches of compost or organic matter and incorporate 2 pounds of a complete lawn or garden fertilizer (15-5-10, 13-13-13, and so forth) per 100 square feet of bed or every 35 feet of row before planting. On small plots, use 2 teaspoons per square foot or foot of row. The ideal soil pH for growing summer squash is 6.0 to 7.0.

How to Plant

Create a raised row about 6 inches high and 12 inches wide. Multiple rows should be around 36 inches apart. Summer squash seed should be planted in groups of seed every 3 to 4 feet. This is known as planting in hills. Open a shallow depression about 1½ to 2 inches deep and 4 inches wide with a hoe. Drop three to four

seeds evenly spaced apart in the hole and cover lightly with loose soil using a hoe or garden rake. Tamp gently with the back of the hoe and water.

Care and Maintenance

As soon as your squash start to bloom, sprinkle 3 tablespoons of a high-nitrogen fertilizer (21-0-0, and so forth) around each hill, being careful to keep it off the plants. Work the fertilizer into the soil lightly with a hoe or rake and water. After side-dressing, applying a layer of organic mulch (hay, straw, grass clippings, and so forth) to conserve water and prevent weeds is ideal. The most common pest problems on squash are cucumber beetles, squash bugs, vine borers, powdery mildew, and virus. Control the insects as they occur with appropriately labeled insecticides. There is no cure for a virus, but controlling the cucumber beetles will help lessen its occurrence.

Harvest

Summer squash is generally ready to pick forty to fifty days after seeding. It's very important to pick summer squash while its skin is tender and before the seeds become hard. Pick yellow squash when it is 4 to 6 inches long or smaller, patty pan (scallop) when 2 to 4 inches in diameter, and zucchini when 6 to 8 inches long. Remember, there is no such thing as a squash too small to eat. Baby squash are succulent and delicious. On the other hand, large, tough squash belong in the compost pile or the feed lot.

Additional Information

Recommended summer squash varieties for Texas include 'Classic' (zucchini), 'Cougar' (yellow), 'Dixie' (yellow), 'Early White Bush' (patty pan), 'Elite' (zucchini), 'Goldie' (yellow), 'Gold Bar' (yellow), 'Hyrific' (yellow), 'Multipik' (yellow), 'Peter Pan' (patty pan), 'President' (zucchini), 'Sunburst' (yellow), 'Senator' (zucchini), and 'Seneca' (zucchini). Summer squash originated in the southwestern United States.

SWEET CORN

If a home gardener needed a reason to live each year, then surely it would be to harvest and eat fresh sweet corn (*Zea mays*). Partaking of it is downright next to sinful. Sweet corn is an all-American crop and should be enjoyed by all Americans. The most important things to remember about growing sweet corn are to plant it in multiple rows to ensure full pollination, to harvest it before it becomes overly mature, and to cook and prepare it as soon after harvest as possible.

When to Plant

In Texas, it's important to plant sweet corn as soon as possible after the last frost in your region but not before. Planting too soon while the soils are cold will result in rotted seed. However, if you wait too long after the last frost, you will most likely have to deal with dry conditions and a poor harvest.

Where to Plant

Sweet corn requires at least eight hours of direct sun each day for maximum production. It isn't picky about soils as long as they drain well. Ideally, till in several inches of compost or organic matter and incorporate 2 pounds of a complete lawn or garden fertilizer (15-5-10, 13-13-13, and so forth) per 100 square feet of bed or every 35 feet of row before planting. The ideal soil pH for growing sweet corn is 6.0 to 7.0.

How to Plant

Sweet corn seed is generally planted 1 to 1½ inches deep in rows that are 30 to 42 inches apart with the seeds 3 to 4 inches apart. I often plant seeds several inches apart to ensure a good stand. Once a good stand is established, thin the plants to around 8 to 12 inches apart.

Care and Maintenance

Sweet corn is a grass and fairly easy to grow if you follow the basic rules of growing grass. It requires regular moisture of about 1 inch of water per week. It also requires high fertility, so it's important to apply additional high-nitrogen fertilizer (21-0-0, and so forth) several times during the growth of the plant for maximum production. Use about ½ cup per 35 feet of row, sprinkled lightly down each side of the row. Do not get it on the plant, however. This should be done when the plants are about 6 inches high and again at about waist high, or half grown. It's important that sweet corn foliage be dark green, never yellow-green, which indicates a nitrogen deficiency. The main pest for sweet corn is the corn earworm, which will eat the kernels off the top of the ear while inside the husk. They can be controlled by regularly keeping *Bacillus thuringiensis* (*Bt,* Dipel, Thuricide) sprinkled or sprayed on the plants and ears. Earworms are inevitable. Just cut off the tops of the ears when shucking and appreciate the fact that they are organically grown. My friend and mentor, Dr. Jerry Parsons, always said any ear of corn without worms is obviously covered with pesticides!

Harvest

Pick ears that feel full in the shucks and have silks that are golden brown to medium brown. If left on the plant until the shucks completely dry to a dark brown color, the corn will be tough and starchy. Cook and serve immediately for the best flavor.

Additional Information

Recommended sweet corn varieties for Texas include 'Merit' (yellow), 'Kandy Korn' (yellow), 'How Sweet It Is' (yellow), 'Silver Queen' (white), and my all-time favorite, 'Sweet G-90' (bi-colored). Did you know that every silk on an ear of corn leads to a kernel and that an ear of corn always has an even number of rows? Sweet corn originated in South America.

SWEET PEPPER

I'm pretty much a gringo when it comes to eating hot peppers, but I sure do love the sweet, mild ones. I like to cook every dish with bell peppers (*Capsicum annuum*) and eat every meal with fresh banana peppers. I love pickled banana peppers too. Except for my favorite bell pepper—'Tequila', which starts out purple—most peppers begin their lives green or yellow and ripen to beautiful shades of gold, orange, and red. Once they turn color, they are even sweeter, more flavorful, and better for you, as the levels of vitamins C and A go way up.

When to Plant

Sweet peppers are warm-weather plants and are planted from transplants well after all danger of frost in the spring. They cannot tolerate a frost or a freeze and thrive with mild and moderately warm temperatures in spring and early summer. Often summer heat and drought kill spring-planted sweet peppers in Texas. By planting transplants again three to four months before the first expected killing freeze in your area, you can successfully grow a fall crop. Sweet pepper plants should be spaced 18 to 24 inches apart.

Where to Plant

Like hot peppers, sweet peppers require at least eight hours of direct sun each day for maximum production. They too require rich, loamy soils that

drain well. Ideally, till in several inches of compost or organic matter and incorporate 2 pounds of a complete lawn or garden fertilizer (15-5-10, 13-13-13, and so forth) per 100 square feet of bed or every 35 feet of row before planting. For smaller plots, use 2 teaspoons per square foot or foot of row. The ideal soil pH for growing sweet peppers is 5.5 to 7.5.

How to Plant

Sweet pepper transplants should be planted in well-cultivated soil. Dig holes that are the same size as the existing pots they are growing in. Gently firm the soil around them. Water thoroughly with a water-soluble plant food such as Miracle-Gro at half the labeled recommendation.

Care and Maintenance

Sweet peppers grow and produce fruit best when the temperatures are warm but below 80 degrees. About three weeks after transplanting, fertilize them with 1 cup of high-nitrogen fertilizer (21-0-0, and so forth) for each 35 feet of row. Sprinkle half of the fertilizer down each side of the row. Lightly work it into the soil and then water. Repeat this fertilizing process every three weeks to keep the plants vigorous. The main pest problems on peppers are leaf miners, spider mites, nematodes, and foliage diseases. If they occur, treat with an appropriately labeled pesticide.

Harvest

Depending on the variety, you should pick sweet peppers sixty-five to eighty days after transplanting them into the garden. Sweet peppers can be harvested at any size but are the sweetest and most flavorful when they reach full maturity. Green peppers that turn red generally taste sweeter and are much higher in vitamin A. Be careful picking the peppers, as the plants are brittle and prone to breaking off. It's actually best to cut the peppers from the plant with a sharp knife or hand pruners. Wash, prepare, or refrigerate them immediately.

Additional Information

Recommended sweet pepper varieties for Texas include 'Bell Tower' (bell), 'Big Bertha' (bell), 'Grande Rio 66' (bell), 'Jupiter' (bell), 'Shamrock' (bell), 'Summer Sweet' hybrids (bell), 'Tequila' (bell), 'Valley Giant' (bell), 'Gypsy' (bell), 'Large Red Cherry', and 'Sweet Banana'. Sweet peppers are native to Central America.

SWEET POTATO

I grew up attending the Yamboree in Gilmer, Texas, where everyone celebrated the yam's contribution to the local economy. Unfortunately, yams aren't produced in Gilmer, Texas, or the United States for that matter. What many folks call yams in the South are actually sweet potatoes (*Ipomoea batatas*). True yams are a tropical root crop not related to sweet potatoes. The African name *yam* came in with the slave trade, and since sweet potatoes were similar in cultivation and preparation, the name was transferred to them. Sweet potatoes by any name belong in every Texas garden and on every Texas table.

When to Plant

Sweet potatoes are a warm-season crop that cannot tolerate frosts or freezes. They can't even stand cool days or nights. The vining plants thrive on heat, so they should be planted well after the last frost in your region. This is generally March in the southern half of the state and April or later in the northern half of the state. Sweet potatoes are planted from slips, or rooted cuttings. These are often available from feed stores and mail-order nurseries. Plant the slips 12 to 16 inches apart.

Where to Plant

Sweet potatoes require at least eight hours of direct sun each day for maximum yields. They do best in well-drained sandy and loamy soils and are best planted in raised beds or rows at least 6 to 12 inches high. Ideally, till in several inches of compost or organic matter and incorporate 1 pound of a complete lawn or garden fertilizer (15-5-10, 13-13-13, and so forth) per 100 square feet of bed or every 35 feet of row before planting. In smaller plantings use 1 teaspoon per square foot or foot of row. The ideal soil pH for growing sweet potatoes is 5.5 to 6.5.

How to Plant

Plant sweet potatoes in raised beds or rows 6 inches high, 18 inches wide, and 36 inches apart. Using a trowel, make holes for the slips every 12 to 16 inches down the row. Place the rooted cuttings in the ground with only the upper leaves above the ground. Water them in with a half-strength water-soluble fertilizer such as Miracle-Gro before covering them with well-cultivated soil. Water them again to eliminate any air pockets.

Care and Maintenance

Sweet potatoes have few problems and are easy to grow as long as they have heat and sunshine, and regular irrigation. About four weeks after planting,

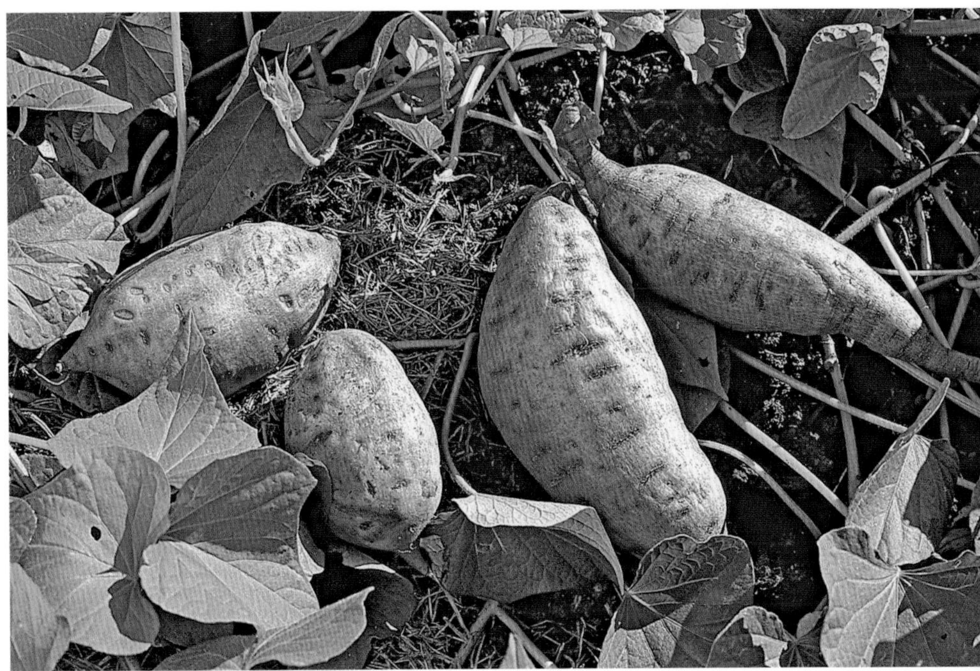

side-dress them with a complete garden fertilizer (13-13-13, 10-20-10, and so forth) at ½ pound per 35 feet of row. Apply to both sides of the row, work the fertilizer into the surface of the soil, and water lightly.

Harvest

Sweet potatoes are generally ready to dig out in 90 to 110 days. They don't actually mature but are dug when they reach a usable size. It's always best to inspect the base of a few plants to check their size before digging them. If they are too small, leave them so they have more time to grow. When the soil is dry, use a shovel to dig out the entire root system carefully. Be careful not to damage the sweet potatoes. Cut the roots away from the plants and allow them to dry for three to four hours in the shade before placing them in a warm, humid area to cure for two weeks. Use your garage or shed, and place them in containers covered with moist burlap. They should then store for three months if they're kept in a cool place (55 degrees).

Additional Information

Recommended sweet potato varieties for Texas include 'Beauregard', 'Centennial', and 'Jewel'. I grow a white-fleshed variety named 'White Triumph'. It's my summer Irish potato. Sweet potatoes originated in Central and South America.

SWISS CHARD

I didn't grow up growing or eating Swiss chard (*Beta vulgaris*, Cicla Group). As a matter of fact, I didn't grow my first crop until I was in a vegetable production class at Texas A&M. Swiss chard is easy to grow and nutritious. Some folks like it better than all other greens, including my dad. Swiss chard is basically a beet without the edible root. It comes in an amazing array of colors and also makes a good ornamental bedding or pot plant. Just remember that it's a cool-season crop, so be sure and grow it during the fall, mild winters, and early spring.

When to Plant

Swiss chard is a cool-weather plant that generally dies when the weather is hot, though it can occasionally survive a summer. For the greens to be tasty and productive however, the temperatures must be cool. Swiss chard can tolerate frosts but not hard freezes and should be planted in late winter or early spring for an initial crop. A second fall crop can be planted around September in the northern half of Texas, and October in the southern half of Texas. Swiss chard can either be direct seeded or planted as transplants, which are often available from garden centers. Once the seedlings are established and have their first true leaves, thin them to (or plant the transplants) 4 to 6 inches apart.

Where to Plant

Swiss chard requires at least eight hours of direct sun each day but can tolerate a bit of filtered light, or as little as five to six hours of direct sun. Plant Swiss chard in rich well-drained soil, either in the ground or in containers at least 12 inches in diameter, preferably larger. It is ideal to till several inches of organic matter into the soil and apply 1 pound of a complete lawn and garden fertilizer (15-5-10, 13-13-13, and so forth) per 100 square feet of bed or every 35 feet of row. In small plots use 1 teaspoon per square foot or foot of row. The ideal pH for growing Swiss chard is 6.0–7.0.

How to Plant

Swiss chard can be grown either in beds or rows 2 to 3 feet apart. To improve seedling germination (sprouting) soak the seed in water overnight at room temperature. Open a shallow trench in your raised row 1 inch deep with the corner of a hoe or a stick. Drop the seeds one inch apart to ensure a good stand. To prevent the soil from crusting over the sprouting seed, cover with compost or potting soil instead of garden soil. Water gently and carefully (to avoid disturbing the seed) and keep the soil moist until germination occurs. Swiss chard seed may take two to three weeks to sprout in the early spring when the soils are cool but only five to seven days when planted in warmer soils for a fall crop. When the seedlings are up, reduce the *frequency* of watering so that the plants gradually get tougher.

Care and Maintenance

Water and fertility are the most critical issues in growing Swiss chard. Never let the plants get excessively dry. When the plants are 6 inches tall fertilize them with a half cup of high-nitrogen fertilizer (21-0-0, and so forth) for each 35 feet of row. Sprinkle half of the fertilizer down each side of the row. Lightly work it into the soil and then water. The main pest problem on Swiss chard is the foliage-feeding flea beetle, which causes numerous small holes in the foliage. Treat with a safe, labeled insecticide as soon as you notice the first damage.

Harvest

Swiss chard greens are ready to harvest in thirty-five to forty days from seed or less from transplants. Harvest the tender, bug-free foliage when it is less than 6 inches long. Larger leaves will be tougher and less tasty. Wash and refrigerate or prepare them immediately after picking for the best flavor. Like other greens, they can be frozen for later use.

Additional Information

Recommended Swiss chard varieties for Texas include 'Bright Lights', 'Five-Color Silverbeet', 'Fordhook Giant', and 'Rhubarb Chard'. Swiss chard originated in the Mediterranean.

TOMATILLO

Once relatively unknown throughout most of Texas, tomatillos (*Physalis philadelphica* or *Physalis ixocarpa*) are as widespread as Mexican food restaurants now, thanks to Tex-Mex green sauces and salsas. These "little tomatoes" are produced in papery husks that look like Chinese lanterns and are harvested and used in their green, relatively tart state. The culture of tomatillos is very similar to their tomato relatives, but unfortunately they are not as productive. Make sure you get an early start because, like tomatoes, they stop producing during the heat of summer.

When to Plant

Tomatillos are planted from transplants after all danger of frost in the spring. They cannot tolerate a frost or a freeze and thrive with mild and moderately warm temperatures in spring and early summer. Often summer heat and drought kill spring-planted tomatillos in Texas. Planting transplants again four months before the first expected killing freeze in your area means you can successfully grow a fall crop. The transplants should be planted 36 to 48 inches apart.

Where to Plant

Like their tomato cousins, tomatillos require at least eight hours of direct sun each day for best yields. They perform best in rich, loamy soils. Ideally, till in several inches of compost or organic matter and incorporate 2 pounds of a complete lawn or garden fertilizer (15-5-10, 13-13-13, and so forth) per 100 square feet of bed or every 35 feet of row before planting. In small plantings incorporate 2 teaspoons per square foot or foot of row. The ideal soil pH for growing tomatillos is 6.0 to 7.0.

How to Plant

Tomatillo transplants should be planted in well-cultivated soil. Dig holes that are the same size as the existing pot they are growing in. Gently firm the soil around them. Water thoroughly with a water-soluble plant food at half the labeled recommendation.

Care and Maintenance

Tomatillos grow and set fruit best when the temperatures are warm but below 80 degrees. Like their tomato cousins, tomatillos benefit from staking or caging to keep them off the ground. About three weeks after transplanting, fertilize them with 1 cup of high-nitrogen fertilizer (21-0-0, and so forth) for each 35 feet of row. Sprinkle half of the fertilizer down each side of the row. Lightly work it into the soil and then water. Repeat this fertilizing process every three weeks to keep the plants vigorous. On smaller plantings use 1 tablespoon of high-nitrogen fertilizer sprinkled around each plant. Tomatillos have few insect or disease problems, but often fail to set good crops of fruit in Texas due to heat and stress.

Harvest

Tomatillos generally ripen around sixty-five to seventy days from transplanting. The fruit is ripe when the light brown papery husk has opened to reveal the plump berry. Ripe fruit often falls to the ground. The riper the fruit, the sweeter they will taste. Wash and prepare, or store in a cool area immediately.

Additional Information

The recommended tomatillo variety for Texas is 'Toma Verde'. Tomatillos originated in Mexico and Central America and are sometimes known as Mexican husk tomatoes. There are purple varieties as well.

TOMATO

I'm embarrassed to admit that I'm not a rabid tomato (*Lycopersicon esculentum*) eater. Sure, I eat them on hamburgers and in spaghetti sauce, but I'm not sure I ever actually purchased one from a grocery store. Of course, the biggest reason is that those from the grocery store are barely edible! The only time of the year that I eat fresh tomatoes is when I grow them in the garden. And I grow plenty of them. Although I'm not a tomato lover, I come from a family who is in love with tomatoes. It's always been my job to keep the relationship healthy. Of course, I'm happy eating easy-to-grow cherry, plum, and other small, fruited tomatoes, but my family wants big slicing types.

When to Plant

Tomatoes are planted from transplants after all danger of frost in the spring. They cannot tolerate frosts or freezes and thrive with mild and moderately warm temperatures in spring and early summer. Tomatoes do not set fruit in the heat of Texas summers (above 92 degrees), which leaves only a small window of opportunity in the spring to form fruit. This makes planting time critical. If you plant too soon, frost will kill them. However, if you plant too late, you severely reduce your production. Therefore, as soon as the last frost occurs in your area, plan on getting your tomato transplants in the ground. The ideal transplant is 6 to 8 inches tall, dark green, and has six to eight healthy leaves. Avoid those that are yellow-green, purple-green, or tough and woody. These are stunted and will not produce a bountiful harvest. To avoid unexpected late frosts, many Texas gardeners have buckets, hot caps, or row cover ready for protecting their plants. Often summer heat and drought kill spring-planted tomatoes in Texas. Planting transplants again four months before the first expected killing freeze in your area means you can successfully grow a fall crop. This timing is crucial to ensure the harvest of ripe fruit, instead of green ones, before frost. Water at this time of year is also critical to their survival. The transplants should be spaced 36 to 48 inches apart.

Where to Plant

Tomatoes require at least eight hours of direct sun each day for maximum yields. If you can't sunbathe there, you can't grow tomatoes, or many other

vegetables for that matter. Tomatoes do best in rich, loamy soils. Due to a problem with root-infecting microscopic nematodes, it is best to avoid areas where this has been a problem or where tomatoes have grown the previous year. Ideally, till in several inches of compost or organic matter and incorporate 2 pounds of a complete lawn or garden fertilizer (15-5-10, 13-13-13, and so forth) per 100 square feet of bed or every 35 feet of row before planting. In small plantings incorporate 2 teaspoons per square foot or foot of row. Many successful tomato growers add a little extra something below the planting hole, including animal manures, cottonseed meal, slow-release fertilizer, and Epsom salt. The ideal soil pH for growing tomatoes is 6.0 to 7.0.

How to Plant

Tomato transplants should be planted in well-cultivated soil. Dig holes twice as wide and at least as deep as the existing pots the tomatoes are growing in. Tomatoes can form roots along their stem so tall plants should have the lower several inches of their stems buried beneath the soil. By planting them deeper, you produce a stronger plant with more roots. Strip any foliage off the lower stem that is to be beneath the ground and place into the hole. Gently firm the soil around them. Water thoroughly with a water-soluble plant food such as Miracle-Gro at half the labeled recommendation. Many successful organic gardeners use manure tea for this.

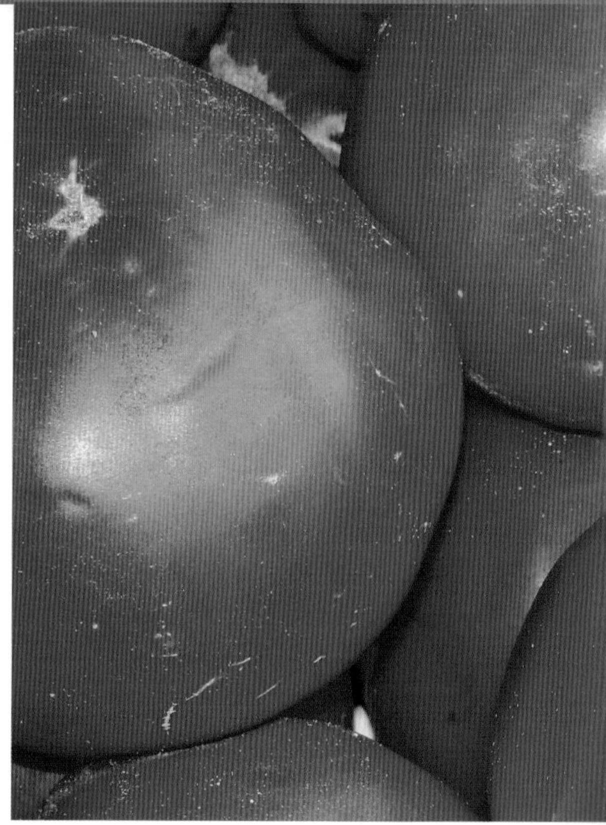

Care and Maintenance

Tomatoes grow and set fruit only when the temperatures are warm but below 92 degrees. About three weeks after transplanting, fertilize them with 1 cup of high-nitrogen fertilizer (21-0-0, and so forth) for each 35 feet of row. Sprinkle half of the fertilizer down each side of the row. Lightly work it into the soil and then water. Repeat this fertilizing process every two to three weeks to keep the plants vigorous. If you only have a few plants, use 2 to 3 teaspoons sprinkled around (but not on) each plant. Be sure to work it lightly into the soil and water the plants well afterward.

Tomatoes are ranked into two different categories, depending on their growth habits. Determinant tomatoes ('Amelia', 'Top Gun', 'Florida 91', 'Floralina', and so forth) form a bush about 36 inches high and set a lot of fruit at the same time. They do well in Texas because, if planted early enough, they set and ripen plenty of tomatoes before the heat of summer causes them to suffer or die. Determinant varieties still need to be staked but don't have to be picked from a ladder. Indeterminate varieties ('Better Boy', 'Champion', 'Super Fantastic', and so forth) continue growing taller all summer and have to be staked or caged to keep them from lying on the ground. They set a few fruit, then grow, and then set a few more fruit and grow some more. Production is usually less on indeterminate varieties, especially if planted late, because like all varieties, they stop setting fruit when it's hot. Some varieties deemed semideterminant (such as 'Celebrity') grow at heights in between.

Caged tomatoes produce more higher-quality fruit, and they have fewer disease problems. The best of all supports for tomatoes are sturdy homemade circular cages made from concrete reinforcing wire. They should be 60 inches high and 20 inches in diameter. It is best to tie them to two stakes hammered into the ground to prevent tall plants from toppling over. With caging, suckers do not need to be removed from the base of the plants. All foliage is

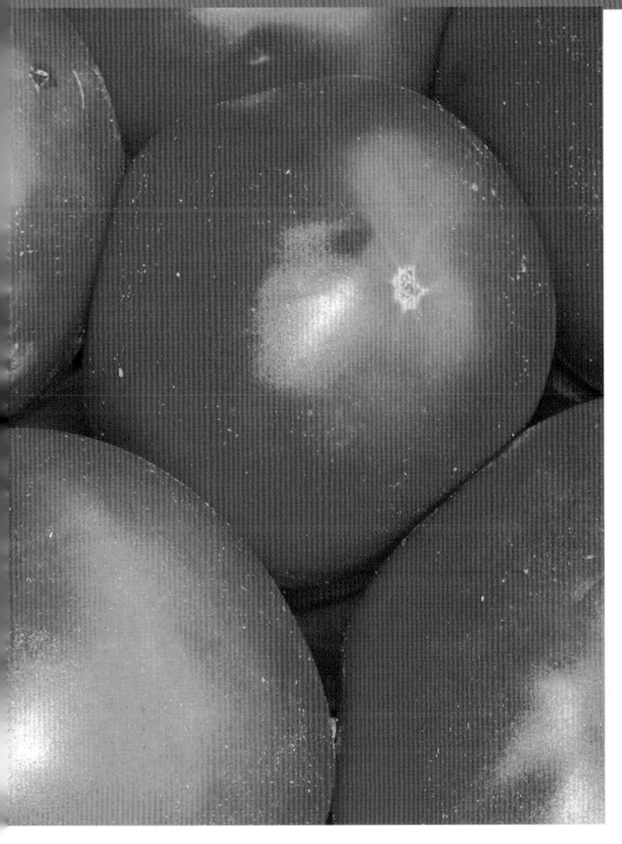

necessary in Texas to keep the tomato fruit from sunburning.

Tomatoes have a host of insect and disease problems, so be prepared. The abbreviations behind the name on the tag tell you what diseases the variety is resistant to. The more you see listed, the better. They include V (verticillium wilt), F (fusarium wilt), N (nematodes), T (tobacco mosaic virus), A (alternaria stem canker), St (stemphylium gray leaf spot), TSWV (tobacco spotted wilt virus), and TYLC (tomato yellow leaf curl).

The worst pest problem on tomatoes is spider mites. They are tiny spider relatives that feed on the underside of the foliage during hot weather and suck the life out of the plants. Severely infested plants will be covered with fine webbing. Spider mites are very serious and should be sprayed with a labeled miticide as soon as they appear.

Harvest

Depending on the variety, tomatoes are generally ready to harvest about seventy to eighty days after transplanting. For eating fresh, harvest the fruit when it is fully colored but still firm. For cooking and canning, you might want to leave them on a bit longer until they're deep red and give a little when you squeeze them. If critters, cracking, or sunburning is a problem, you can pick them when they first start to turn pink and ripen them at room temperature in a shady location. Of course, green tomatoes can be eaten fried or made into relish.

Additional Information

Recommended tomato varieties for Texas include 'Amelia', 'Bush Early Girl', 'Beefmaster', 'Better Boy', 'Better Bush', 'BHN 444', 'BHN 589', 'Celebrity', 'Champion', 'Early Girl', 'Floralina', 'Florida 91', 'Parks Whopper', 'Super Fantastic', and 'Top Gun'. You can never go wrong with 'Celebrity'. Most cherry and small-fruited varieties do well. Tomatoes originated in South America and were once considered toxic.

TURNIP

Yes, I know, turnips (*Brassica rapa*, Rapifera Group) are far from a glamorous vegetable. But I'd make you grow them if I could. They are extremely easy to grow and very nutritious. All you need is cool weather and full sun. My family has eaten many a pot of turnip greens in our life.

When to Plant

Turnips are cool-weather plants that die when the weather is hot. The flavor of turnips gets stronger with heat as well. And like most greens, the texture gets tougher too. Turnips can tolerate frosts but not hard freezes, so they should be planted in late winter or early spring for an initial crop. A second fall crop can be planted around September in the northern half of Texas, and in October in the southern half of Texas. Turnips are easily direct seeded into the garden. Once the seedlings are established, thin them to 3 to 4 inches apart.

Where to Plant

Turnips require at least eight hours of direct sun each day. Like most root crops, they do best in well-drained sandy and loamy soils and are best planted in raised beds or rows at least 6 to 12 inches high. Ideally, till in several inches of compost or organic matter and incorporate 2 pounds of a complete lawn or garden fertilizer (15-5-10, 13-13-13, and so forth) per 100 square feet of

bed or every 35 feet of row before planting. In smaller plantings use 2 teaspoons per square foot or foot of row. The ideal soil pH for growing turnips is 6.0 to 7.0.

How to Plant

Turnips can be grown either in beds or rows 3 feet apart. Open a shallow trench in your raised row ½ inch deep with the corner of a hoe or a stick. Sow the seeds 10 to 12 per foot of row and cover with ¼ to ½ inch of soil. Another option is to sprinkle the seed on top of the row or bed and lightly rake the surface to cover them. After seeding, gently tamp down the soil with the back of your hoe. Water gently and keep the soil moist. With adequate moisture, turnip seedlings can be up in as little as three to four days. When the seedlings are up, reduce the *frequency* of watering so that the plants toughen. In order for turnip roots to form properly, it's critical that the seedlings be thinned once they have been up around seven days.

Care and Maintenance

Turnips are extremely easy to grow. When grown for roots, there's generally no need for an additional application of fertilizer. However, for continuous greens production apply ½ cup of a high nitrogen-fertilizer (21-0-0, and so forth) for each 35 feet of row after the first harvest. Adding a layer of organic mulch (straw, hay, and so forth) around them is ideal. They have few pest problems, with foliage-feeding flea beetles being the worst.

Harvest

Turnip greens can be harvested as few as thirty days after seeding while turnip roots generally take around sixty days. Some gardeners harvest the pest-free, oldest (but still tender), lower leaves one at a time by hand, while others cut off the entire plant just above the base. Remember to pick them often to keep producing tender leaves. Older leaves will get bitter and tough. Turnips roots are edible at any stage but are generally harvested when they are 1 to 3 inches in diameter. They should be washed and prepared or refrigerated immediately. They will keep for several weeks in a plastic bag in the refrigerator.

Additional Information

Recommended turnip varieties for Texas include 'All Top' (greens only), 'Purple Top White Globe', 'Royal Globe II', 'Seven Top' (greens only), 'Shogoin', 'Tokyo Cross', 'White Globe', and 'White Lady'. The Chinese cultivated turnips in 200 B.C., and they were also cultivated by the early Romans. They are native to western Asia.

WATERMELON

Watermelons (*Citrullus lanatus*) are celebrated with festivals throughout Texas and the South. They have been a lifesaving treat for man and beast for thousands of years. They are refreshing, sweet, and nutritious. Several ingredients are necessary for growing good watermelons. These include loose, sandy soil, plenty of room, and full sun.

When to Plant

Watermelons require warm soils to germinate and should be planted after all danger of frost in the spring. They are generally direct seeded into the garden but occasionally available as transplants from garden centers. Once the seedlings are established, they should be thinned to (or transplants planted) 4 to 6 feet apart.

Where to Plant

Watermelons require at least eight hours of direct sun each day for maximum yields. They do best in well-drained sandy and loamy soils. Ideally, till in several inches of compost or organic matter and incorporate 2 pounds of a complete lawn or garden fertilizer (15-5-10, 13-13-13, and so forth) per 100 square feet of bed or every 35 feet of row before planting. The ideal soil pH for growing watermelons is 6.0 to 7.0.

How to Plant

Create a raised row about 6 inches high and 12 inches wide. Multiple rows should be around 6 feet apart. Watermelon seed should be planted in groups of seed every 4 to 6 feet. This is known as planting in hills. Open a shallow depression ¾ to 1 inch deep and 4 inches wide with a hoe. Drop three to four seeds evenly spaced apart in the hole and cover lightly with loose soil using a hoe or garden rake. Gently tamp down with the back of your hoe.

Care and Maintenance

As soon as the vines on the watermelon start to run (vine), you need to apply an additional application of fertilizer. Sprinkle 3 tablespoons of a high-nitrogen fertilizer, such as ammonium sulfate (21-0-0), around each hill, being careful to keep it off the plants. Work the fertilizer into the soil lightly with a hoe or rake and water. After fertilizing, applying a layer of organic mulch (hay, straw, grass clippings, and so forth) to conserve water and prevent weeds is ideal. Generally diseases are more of a problem on watermelons than insects. Be on the lookout for downy mildew, gummy stem blight, fusarium wilt, virus, and nematodes. All are difficult to control.

Harvest

Most watermelon varieties ripen in eighty to ninety days. No fruit or vegetable causes more consternation than the question of when to pick a watermelon. First of all, it should be normal shaped for the variety. Deformed watermelons never ripen properly and should be picked off and discarded. Secondly, the tendril nearest the watermelon should be brown and withered. Next, check the underside of the melon that is touching the ground. It should have turned from white to cream or yellowish colored. And finally there's the watermelon thump. If it's too green, it will make a high-pitched sound. If it's overripe, it will make a low, dull thud. I once heard a Japanese watermelon breeder explain it in these useful terms. Thumping an underripe watermelon sounds the same as thumping your forehead. Thumping a ripe watermelon sounds more like thumping your chest. And thumping and overripe melon sounds like thumping your stomach. Give it a try. Some farmers and gardeners pat the melons with their hand instead of thumping for the same sounds.

Additional Information

Recommended watermelon varieties for Texas include 'All Sweet', 'Black Diamond', 'Charleston Gray', 'Crimson Sweet', 'Jamboree', 'Jubilee', 'Mickeylee' (small fruited), 'Olé', 'Royal Charleston', 'Royal Jubilee', 'Royal Peacock', 'Royal Sweet', 'Sangria', 'Sentinel', 'Tendersweet' (yellow meat), 'King of Hearts' (seedless), 'Millennium' (seedless), 'Seedless Sweet Heart' (seedless), 'Sweet Slice' (seedless), 'Tri-X 313' (seedless), and 'Triple Crown' (seedless). Watermelons originated in Africa.

WINTER SQUASH

Though I grew up primarily growing and dining on summer squash, I have always been fascinated by the plethora of diversity in winter squash (*Cucurbita maxima*).There are so many different kinds and colors that they almost make decorating with pumpkins in the fall seem dull. They are also good to eat and good for you. And unlike summer squash, these hard-shelled ornaments last for months with no refrigeration. Most of them grow on large, spreading vines, so remember to give them plenty of room in the garden and on the table.

When to Plant

Winter squash require warm soils to germinate and should be planted in the spring after all danger of frost has passed (generally April in the northern half of Texas and March in the southern half). It cannot tolerate frost or freezes. To produce a fall crop of winter squash for eating and decorating, plant the seed approximately three to four months (generally around July) before the first killing frost in your area. Different varieties have a different number of days to maturity so be sure to check the variety description and add about 25 days for slower maturity in the fall. Winter squash is easily direct seeded into the garden. Once the seedlings are established and have their first true leaves, thin them to 36 to 48 inches apart.

Where to Plant

Winter squash requires at least eight hours of direct sun each day for maximum production. It isn't picky about soils as long as they drain well.

Ideally, till in several inches of compost or organic matter and incorporate 2 pounds of a complete lawn or garden fertilizer (15-5-10, 13-13-13, and so forth) per 100 square feet of bed or every 35 feet of row before planting. On smaller plots, use 2 teaspoons per square foot or foot of row. The ideal soil pH for growing winter squash is 6.0 to 7.0.

How to Plant

Create a raised row about 6 inches high and 12 inches wide. Multiple rows should be around 8 feet apart. Squash seed should be planted in groups of seed every 6 feet. This is known as planting in hills. Open a shallow depression about 1 inch deep and 4 inches wide with a hoe. Drop four to five seeds evenly spaced apart in the hole and cover lightly with loose soil using a hoe or garden rake.

Care and Maintenance

When the first blooms appear, sprinkle 3 tablespoons of a high0nnitrogen fertilizer (21-0-0, and so forth) around each hill, being careful to keep it off the plants. Work the fertilizer into the soil lightly with a hoe or rake and water. After side-dressing, applying a layer of organic mulch (hay, straw, grass clippings, and so forth) to conserve water and prevent weeds is ideal. The most common pest problems on squash are cucumber beetles, squash bugs, vine borers, powdery mildew, and virus. Control the insects as they occur with appropriately labeled insecticides. There is no cure for the virus, but controlling the cucumber beetles will help lessen its occurrence.

Harvest

Depending on the variety, winter squash is normally ready to harvest 70 to 100 days after planting the seed. Winter squash should not be harvested until the rinds are hard and cannot be scratched with your fingernail. Like their pumpkin kin, winter squash fruit can tolerate frosts but not hard freezes, so be sure to bring them into storage before the first killing freeze. To store them, brush off the dirt (do not wash) and place them in a single layer in a cool dry area where they will keep for four to six months.

Additional Information

Recommended winter squash varieties for Texas include 'Table Ace' (acorn), 'Early Butternut', 'Table King' (acorn), 'Vegetable Spaghetti', and 'Waltham' (butternut). Winter squash originated in the southwestern United States.

FRUITS

Everybody likes sugar. Heck, I'm part hummingbird. But we all know that refined sugars aren't good for us. Overdosing on sugar is a recipe for obesity and diabetes. Luckily, nature provides us her own candy in the form of fruits. Home grown fruit can give us our sugar fix, plus a bonus of antioxidants, fiber, and exercise while producing it. Of course fruits are also a good way to introduce vegetable-hating youngsters to the world of nutritious produce.

Before you get all excited about stocking your own home fruit stand, you must first realize that we are limited in what we can produce in Texas. Some fruits, like apricots, black raspberries, and kiwis, are essentially impossible to produce here. Others, like apples, blueberries, and peaches, require lots of preparation, maintenance, and tending. But just about anybody can grow blackberries, figs, and pears if you choose the right types.

And of course fresh fruit means fresh eating, cobblers, ice cream, pies, jellies, jams, and preserves. Eating your own home grown vegetables is satisfying and fulfilling, but

eating your own fresh-picked fruit is downright extravagant. Unfortunately, growing your own fruit is trickier than growing your own veggies. It requires thought, homework, and follow-through. I suggest that you locate living producing examples of what you want to produce before you attempt it. Variety selection is everything in home fruit production. It's also extremely important that you follow the recommended "recipe" for producing each crop. Many Texas gardeners have wasted loads of time and money on fruitful pipe dreams because they didn't think it through or follow it through. You'll do better.

APPLE

Until I tasted delicious fresh-picked apples (*Malus pumila* or *M. domestica*) from the Love Creek Ranch orchard in Medina years ago, I had always considered producing apples in Texas impossible. Sure, there were rumors of their production in the far northern reaches of the state, but I'd never actually seen one, much less eaten one. I'll be the first to admit that we can't produce a shiny Washington State 'Red Delicious' lookalike here, but as I found out, a fresh-picked apple of any color tastes better than one from storage. My professor told us in college that nothing but a 'Red Delicious' apple would ever sell, but as you can see by the selection in the produce section today, tastier multicolored apples are the rage. Thanks to new varieties that don't require cold winters, we, too, can now grow apples.

When to Plant

Apple trees are generally planted during the winter or early spring. Although occasionally available bare root, most are grown and sold as grafted containerized plants. If you are planting bare-root apples, it is absolutely a must that you plant them when they are dormant during the winter. Containerized plants can be planted year-round, with fall being the best time, winter second best, spring third best, and summer the worst. They should be spaced about 10 to 20 feet apart.

Where to Plant

Apples require full sun of at least eight hours a day (preferably more) to produce well. They can be grown in most soils but prefer those that are fertile and well drained. Most apples require cold winters; therefore, they do better the further north you are in Texas. The ideal soil pH for apples is between 6.0 to 6.5.

How to Plant

Dig a hole twice as wide as the tree's rootball and as deep as the taproot or pot it was in. Water the rootball in the hole and then backfill the lower three-fourths of the hole with the native soil and the upper one-fourth with a mixture of the native soil and compost. Be careful not to plant the tree too deep or it will die. Create a circular berm around the tree that acts as a catch basin for water, and water the tree once a week until it's established. A berm is a buildup of soil that creates a small dividing hill between the tree and the rest of your garden. Most berms are no higher than 18 to 24 inches.

Care and Maintenance

When your apple trees are young and developing, you will want to thin the branches so that they are evenly spaced apart. This will include removing the centermost branch or central leader and any overly vigorous suckers or water sprouts. Also remove any dead branches. For the first three years of the trees' lives, apply ½ pound of a complete garden fertilizer (13-13-13, 10-20-10, and so forth) in the spring and again in the fall each year. Mature trees don't require much fertilizer, but if they make less than 6 inches of growth each year, apply 1 pound of a complete garden fertilizer for each 1 inch of trunk diameter. Make sure they get approximately 1 to 2 inches of water per week either through rainfall or irrigation. Apples are susceptible to mites, apple scab, bitter rot, and fire blight. Each should be controlled with an appropriately labeled pesticide before they become a serious problem.

Harvest

In Texas, apples generally don't produce their characteristic red color and may be on the greenish side. Once they have reached full size, they can be ripened off the tree if need be.

Additional Information

Apples require at least two different trees that are known to pollinate each other. Recommended varieties for Texas include 'Anna', 'Braeburn', 'Dorsett Golden', 'Ein Sheimer', 'Fuji', 'Gala', 'Granny Smith', 'Jersey Mac', 'Mollies Delicious' (my favorite), and 'Starkrimson Red Delicious'. Apples originated in Turkey.

BLACKBERRY

Many of us grew up picking blackberries (*Rubus fruticosus*) in the country. My maternal grandmother would lead us on a trek to fencerows and unmowed pastures to harvest the plump dark delicacies. Around our house they were mostly made into delicious cobblers and jelly. Texas isn't known for being able to produce a plethora of fruits, but we can certainly grow blackberries well. Thanks to extremely productive, upright, and even thornless varieties, almost anybody in the state with a bit of room and sunshine can harvest their own at home now. The most important thing to know is that they produce on last year's canes, which die to the ground after producing.

When to Plant

Blackberries are generally planted as 1-gallon containerized plants. Occasionally they may be purchased bare root, loosely packed in bags or pots, or even as dormant root cuttings. Without a doubt, fully-rooted containerized plants are the way to go and will get you into the blackberry-eating business sooner. As with most containerized plants in Texas, the best time to plant is fall, followed by winter, spring, and lastly summer. Planting at the beginning of our cooler, moister season ensures that the plants get established before having to endure our inevitable summer droughts. Blackberries make fairly large plants, as high as 5 feet tall, and should be planted 3 feet apart.

Where to Plant

Like most fruits, blackberries need at least eight hours of full sun (preferably more) for maximum production. Blackberries prefer slightly acidic, well-drained soils and can tolerate both heat and cold. The ideal soil pH for blackberries is 5.5 to 7.5.

How to Plant

Blackberries were once sold mostly bare root or from root cuttings that had to be planted in the winter when they were dormant. Luckily these days, they are mostly sold growing in containers, which can be planted year-round as long as there is moisture. Dig a hole the same depth but a little wider than the plant, place the rootball into it, and backfill with your existing soil. Put 1 to 2 inches of mulch (compost, pine bark, straw, and so forth) around the plants to prevent weeds, moderate soil temperatures, and conserve moisture.

Care and Maintenance

Apply ¼ pound of a complete lawn or garden fertilizer (13-13-13, 10-20-10, and so forth) per plant in the late winter, before growth begins, and again after fruit harvest in the summer, when the canes are pruned. Blackberries produce fruit on canes that grew the previous year. After fruiting, these canes die and should be cut out and removed using long-handled loppers. Cut the new canes back to between 36 to 48 inches to encourage branching and heavier fruit production the following year.

Harvest

Blackberries will not ripen off the plant and should be picked at the peak of ripeness, when they are the blackest and plumpest, and placed in the refrigerator immediately.

Additional Information

Recommended blackberry varieties for Texas include 'Apache' (thornless), 'Arapaho' (thornless), 'Brazos' (thorny), 'Kiowa' (thorny), 'Navaho' (thornless), 'Quachita' (thornless), and 'Rosborough' (thorny). Though harder to pick, production is higher on the thorny varieties. Blackberries are native to North America. Unfortunately, true raspberries do not grow or produce well (or at all) in Texas.

BLUEBERRY

Rabbiteye blueberries (*Vaccinium ashei*) require very acidic, well-drained soils and regular moisture, so their cultivation in the ground is limited to the Pineywoods of East Texas. They can be grown in large whiskey barrel–sized containers in other parts of the state, however. They are relatively pest free, have pretty fall foliage, and have fruit that is loaded with healthy antioxidants. Water quality is an issue with blueberry plants. They do not tolerate alkaline or salty water. This is one more reason for those who call Texas home to have a cistern and collect runoff rainwater from their roofs.

When to Plant

Blueberries are grown in containers and can be planted any time of the year when moisture is available. As with all container-grown plants, fall planting is best, followed by winter, spring, and finally summer, which can be stressful due to heat and drought.

Where to Plant

Blueberries should be planted in very acidic soils with an ideal pH range of 4.0 to 5.5. The soil should be highly organic and well drained. They are mostly grown in the well-drained, sandy, acid soils of East Texas that are heavily amended with black composted pine bark and sphagnum peat moss. They can also be grown in large, whiskey barrel–sized containers of professional-grade potting soil, or a mixture of one-third washed sand, one-third composted pine bark, and one-third sphagnum peat moss.

How to Plant

To ensure good drainage, dig a hole three-fourths as deep and twice as wide as the plant, place the rootball into it with one-fourth of it sticking up above the soil line, and backfill with a mixture of one-third native soil, one-third composted pine bark, and one-third sphagnum peat moss. Put 3 to 4 inches of composted pine bark or clean pine straw mulch in a circle 2 feet around the plants to prevent weeds, moderate soil temperatures, and conserve moisture. The pine bark mulch or straw will also keep the soil more acidic as it breaks down.

Care and Maintenance

Growing blueberries is basically the same as growing their cousins, azaleas, except they require full sun. Blueberries are sensitive to the type of fertilizer you use, how much and often you apply it, and the irrigation water you provide. Only use special acid-loving azalea-camellia-gardenia fertilizer or ammonium sulfate (21-0-0), as other forms of fertilizer can kill blueberries.

Do not apply any the first year. Starting the second year, apply 1 ounce per plant sprinkled evenly around the plants before applying new mulch in late winter. Never use barnyard fertilizer (manure) on blueberries. Keep them generously mulched each year, especially during summer, with peat moss, pine bark, or pine straw. Blueberries have shallow roots with no root hairs and should be weeded by hand. Blueberries are not very drought tolerant and need the equivalent of 1 to 2 inches of water per week. They cannot tolerate poor drainage and will die if growing in wet muck or heavy clay. If your water source is salty or alkaline, you will need to water them with rainwater.

Harvest

Rabbiteye blueberries do not ripen after they are picked and should be left on the plant until they are plump and dark blue. Otherwise they will be tart. You may need to use bird netting to keep from sharing them with your feathered friends.

Additional Information

Rabbiteye blueberries are not self-fruitful; therefore, you will need to plant at least two different varieties for cross-pollination and fruiting. Recommended rabbiteye blueberry varieties for Texas include 'Briteblue', 'Britewell', 'Climax', 'Delite', 'Powderblue', 'Premier', 'Tifblue', and 'Woodard'. Blueberries are native to North America.

CITRUS

When one thinks of citrus (*Citrus* spp.) production in Texas, of course the Rio Grande Valley comes to mind. After all, Texas is home to the world-famous 'Ruby Red' grapefruit and 'Rio Red' grapefruit, our official state fruit. And in the Valley, it's certainly possible to produce a wide range of tropical citrus. However, a number of types of citrus can take some freezing during mild and moderate winters with almost all citrus being quite suitable to growing in portable container pots. The fragrance of citrus blossoms is so alluring that it's almost worth growing some in pots just to experience their floral aroma.

When to Plant

Citrus is grown in containers and can be planted any time of the year when moisture is available. Since citrus is cold tender, spring planting, after all danger of freezes has past, is recommended.

Where to Plant

Citrus fruits require full sun of at least eight hours a day—preferably more—for maximum production. Citrus can be produced in shadier sites, receiving five to seven hours of sun, but the production will be limited and the trees open and sparsely branched. Citrus fruits can be grown in most soils but prefer those that are well drained. In heavy clay soils along the coast, it is best to plant them on slightly raised mounds for increased drainage. Citrus cannot tolerate hard, prolonged freezes so therefore performs best in the lower third of the state, especially along the coast and in the Rio Grande Valley.

How to Plant

Citrus is generally sold growing in 3- or 5-gallon containers. Dig a hole the same depth but a little wider than the pot, place the rootball into it, and backfill with your existing soil. Water well. Put 1 to 2 inches of mulch (compost, pine bark, straw, and so forth) around the plants to prevent weeds, moderate soil temperatures, and conserve moisture. An extra-thick layer of mulch can be placed over the roots and around the trunks during severe cold.

Care and Maintenance

Citrus trees are tough and fairly easy to grow. Freezing temperatures are their worst enemy. Be prepared to move them, cover them, wrap their trunks, or heat them during hard freezes. Some gardeners build frames or cages around their citrus trees to make covering them during the winter easier. Fertilize them in the spring with 1 pound of a complete lawn and garden fertilizer (15-5-10, 13-13-13, and so forth) per inch of trunk diameter. Citrus trees are prone to spider mites, scale, and white flies. Black sooty mold growing on the top of the leaves is a sure sign of scale or white flies. A regular spraying of dormant or summer oil will help control these.

Harvest

Citrus will not ripen off the tree and should be left on until fully sized and colored. 'Satsuma' mandarins should be clipped from the tree to avoid pulling a hunk of peel off when they are harvested.

Additional Information

More cold-hardy species and varieties for the lower half of Texas include 'Changsha' tangerine, 'Kumquat', 'Meyer Lemon', and 'Satsuma' mandarin. Satsumas are my favorite citrus in the world! Lucky folks along the Gulf Coast and in the Rio Grande Valley can grow grapefruit, lemons, limes, sweet oranges, and tangerines. Just remember to share with your friends up north. Citrus fruits are native to Asia.

FIG

One of the many pleasures of spending summers with my grandparents on the farm was picking and eating fresh "sugar figs." Sure the leaves were a bit scratchy, but it was all worth it to find the really soft, sweet ones. Figs (*Ficus carica*) are among the easiest of fruits to grow in Texas, so I say if you don't like them, learn to like them! Unlike most fruit trees in general, figs don't require pruning or pesticide sprays. They just need sun and regular moisture while the figs are ripening. Humans aren't the only ones who crave these sweet treasures. There's always a beautiful red summer tanager in the woods behind the house clamoring for them to get ripe and when they do, he's in there picking as fast as I am. He's no birdbrain.

When to Plant

Figs are normally sold growing in nursery containers and can be planted any time of the year. As they can be a bit tender during very cold winters, it's best to plant them in the early spring so they can get established and hardened off before their first freezing temperatures.

Where to Plant

Figs produce best in full sun with at least eight hours of direct light each day but can survive and produce a fair crop with as little as little as five hours of direct sun daily. Figs will tolerate most soil types as long as they are at least moderately drained, and they can tolerate both acid and alkaline soils.

How to Plant

Dig a hole the same depth but a little wider than the pot, place the rootball into it, and backfill with your existing soil. Water well. Put 1 to 2 inches of mulch (compost, pine bark, straw, and so forth) in a 3- to 4-foot circle around the plants to prevent weeds, moderate soil temperatures, and conserve moisture.

Care and Maintenance

Figs are easy to grow and generally require very little care. It's quite easy to grow them organically in Texas. Because of periodic hard freezes that occasionally kill them to the ground, figs aren't pruned in Texas but are allowed to grow into large shrubs or multitrunked trees. Water them regularly when they are in full fruit to avoid fruit drop. They have few insect and disease problems. However, nematodes can cause trees to be stunted or limit production, and fig rust fungus can cause the foliage to prematurely drop. The figs can also sour during periods of wet, humid weather. Occasionally, entire trees can die from cotton root rot in areas with high pH soils. Figs generally don't require additional fertilizer. Adding compost or mulch around them each year generally provides all the nutrients they need.

Harvest

Figs should be harvested when they are plump, soft, and fully ripe. The ripe color of the fig depends on the variety and can vary from green to yellow, brown, or purple. The riper they get, the sweeter they get. Unfortunately, if you leave them on to long, they will sour and ferment. Birds, raccoons, and possums love figs as well so you might have to cover the entire tree with bird netting from your local garden center. Fig foliage irritates many people's skin, so be prepared to pick your figs wearing long sleeves.

Additional Information

Recommended varieties for Texas include 'Alma', 'Brown Turkey', 'Celeste', and 'Texas Everbearing'. Figs are native to the Middle East and are high in fiber and potassium.

GRAPE

The allure of growing grapes (*Vitis* spp.) in Texas has always presented a major battle between hopeful enthusiasm and stark reality. On the surface you'd think it would be quite easy since Texas is home to many native grape species. But it turns out, thanks to Pierce's disease and birds, growing wine and table grapes in our big state is no small feat. Wine grapes and the common seedless table grapes are from Europe are only adapted to the western and northwestern parts of the state. The rest of the state is better off producing American hybrid grapes, a number of which have native Texas grapes in their blood.

When to Plant

Grapes are mostly grown in containers and can be planted anytime of the year when moisture is available. As with all container-grown plants, fall planting is best, followed by winter, spring, and finally summer, which can be stressful due to heat and drought. Be aware that most nurseries and garden centers stock their fruiting plants during the late winter and early spring.

Where to Plant

Grapes produce best in full sun with at least eight hours of direct light each day. They will tolerate most soil types as long as they are well drained but produce best in deep, sandy loam soil. Grapes can generally tolerate both acid and alkaline soils.

How to Plant

Dig a hole the same depth but a little wider than the pot, place the rootball into it, and backfill with your existing soil. Water well. Put 1 to 2 inches of mulch (compost, pine bark, straw, and so forth) in a 3- to 4-foot circle around the plants to prevent weeds, moderate soil temperatures, and conserve moisture.

Care and Maintenance

Grapes are generally easy to grow. They can, however, be plagued with disease problems, especially in the eastern third of the state where muscadines are a better choice. With high rainfall and humidity, grapes are prone to black rot fungus and the deadly Pierce's disease. They require little to no fertilizer. If the vines are weak or you have deep, sandy soil, apply ¼ pound of a complete lawn and garden fertilizer during late winter. Pruning and training are the biggest chores in grape growing. Visit your county extension agent for complete instructions on the different styles of grape pruning. Do not prune at all the first year. You will need to train them onto a sturdy fence, trellis, or other structure. Grapes produce on old wood and have a tendency to overproduce. Therefore, you must prune them heavily each year, removing about 80 percent of the vines during the winter.

Harvest

Grapes will not ripen off the vine and must be left on until they are fully ripe. For maximum sweetness, pick them when they are plump and fully colored. Refrigerate (or eat them!) immediately.

Additional Information

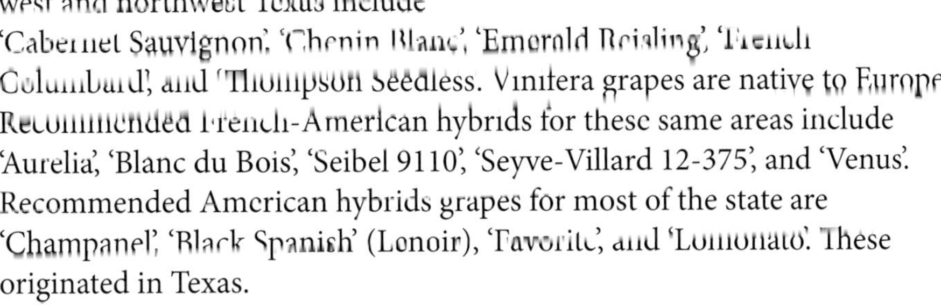

Recommended vinifera (European) grapes for the cooler, drier areas of west and northwest Texas include 'Cabernet Sauvignon', 'Chenin Blanc', 'Emerald Reisling', 'French Columbard', and 'Thompson Seedless'. Vinifera grapes are native to Europe. Recommended French-American hybrids for these same areas include 'Aurelia', 'Blanc du Bois', 'Seibel 9110', 'Seyve-Villard 12-375', and 'Venus'. Recommended American hybrids grapes for most of the state are 'Champanel', 'Black Spanish' (Lenoir), 'Favorite', and 'Lomonato'. These originated in Texas.

LOQUAT

Loquats (*Eriobotrya japonica*) are normally grown as small evergreen ornamental trees in Texas. They are not to be confused with kumquats, a type of citrus. But loquats aren't just useful as ornamentals. They make sweet tasty orange fruit that can be eaten fresh or made into jelly. The fruit's flavor has earned it the common name of Japanese plum over the years. It's not uncommon in the lower half of the state to see large, leafed loquat trees laden with the small, round orange fruit in the spring. The northern half of the state is hit or miss with loquat crops. Some years we have so many of them on the trees at work that we take batting practice with all the ones we don't eat and after winters with hard freezes we have none to eat or play with.

When to Plant

Loquats are normally sold growing in nursery containers and can be planted any time of the year, as long as moisture is available. They can be a bit tender during very cold winters, so it's best to plant them in the early spring to get established and hardened off before their first freezing temperatures.

Where to Plant

Loquats produce best in full sun with at least eight hours of direct light each day but can survive and produce a fair crop with as little as five hours of direct sun daily. Loquats will tolerate most soil types as long as they are at least moderately drained. They can tolerate both acid and alkaline soils.

How to Plant

Dig a hole the same depth but a little wider than the pot, place the rootball into it, and backfill with your existing soil. Water well. Put 1 to 2 inches of mulch (compost, pine bark, straw, and so forth) in a 3- to 4-foot circle around the plants to prevent weeds, moderate soil temperatures, and conserve moisture.

Care and Maintenance

Loquats require very little care and can be grown organically in Texas. The biggest threat to their production is freezing temperatures while they are in bloom during the winter. It's not uncommon for loquats to survive in the northern half of the state but not produce any fruit. In areas with cold winters, consider planting them on the south or west side of your home, or near brick or stone walls and concrete or asphalt surfaces that absorb and release heat during the night. These areas create warm microclimates and extend the hardiness range of semitropical plants. Other than the removal of dead wood, they do not require pruning, spraying, or fertilizing. Fire blight, which causes dead tips on the branches, can occasionally be a problem.

Harvest

To be sweet and juicy, loquats should be harvested when they are plump, fully ripe, and dark orange. If they are picked when they are yellow, they will be tart. Eat, prepare, or refrigerate immediately.

Additional Information

Seedlings and named varieties all do well in Texas. Loquats are native to China and are a member of the rose family.

MAYHAW

This small, fruited hawthorn is an apple relative and produces the famed mayhaw jelly sold throughout the South. Though typically native to swamps, mayhaws (*Crataegus opaca*) can be grown in well-drained garden soils as well. Unfortunately, they prefer acidic soils, which limits their cultivation to the eastern side of Texas where the tall pines grow. Mayhaws earned their name as the fruit generally ripens in May (or a bit before). In the old days, folks would take boats to the swamps and rivers and skim floating mayhaws from the top of the water, somewhat like harvesting similar-looking cranberries. But of course it's much easier to grow one in the yard and shake the tree over a bed sheet when they are ripe.

When to Plant

Mayhaw trees are generally planted during the winter or early spring. Most are grown and sold as containerized plants. Plants from containers can be planted year-round, with fall being the best time, winter second, spring third, and summer the worst. They should be spaced about 15 to 20 feet apart.

Where to Plant

Mayhaws require full sun of at least eight hours a day (preferably more) to produce well. They can be grown in most soils but prefer those that are acidic. Though they are native to boggy swampland, mayhaws do best on well-drained upland sandy loam sites with irrigation. The ideal soil pH for mayhaws is 5.5 to 6.5.

How to Plant

Dig a hole twice as wide as the tree's rootball and as deep as the pot it was in. Water the rootball in the hole and then backfill with the native soil. Be sure not to plant the tree too deep or it will die. Create a circular berm around the tree that acts as a catch basin for water, and water the tree once a week until it's established.

Care and Maintenance

Make sure your mayhaw gets approximately 1 to 2 inches of water per week either through rainfall or irrigation. Mayhaws require little pruning other than to remove any dead branches. For the first three years of the tree's life, give mayhaws a ½-pound application of a complete garden fertilizer (13-13-13, 10-20-10, and so forth) in the spring and again in the fall each year. Mature trees don't require much fertilizer, but if they make less than 6 inches of growth each year, apply 1 pound of a complete garden fertilizer for each inch of trunk diameter. Mayhaws are susceptible to fire blight and especially cedar apple rust, which spots the foliage and deforms the fruit. Avoid planting near cedar trees and clean up all fallen fruit and foliage each year. Avoid wetting the foliage as well.

Harvest

Mayhaws are generally ready to be harvested in April and May, hence the name. Pick them when they are plump and red. When fully ripe, the fruit will fall from the tree. Many mayhaw lovers lay sheets down below the branches and then shake the limbs to catch the fallen fruit. If cedar apple rust is a problem, you might have to pick the fruit early. If it killed you to eat a little cedar apple rust, I'd already be dead.

Additional Information

You'll need to plant two different varieties of mayhaws for cross-pollination and improved fruit set. Recommended mayhaw varieties for Texas include 'Super Berry', 'Super Spur', and 'Texas Star'. Mayhaws are native to North America.

MUSCADINE

Muscadine (*Vitis rotundifolia*) is a nontypical type of grape native to East Texas and the southeastern United States. They can be bronze or purple-black and have large round fruit that grow in loose clusters. Country people in East Texas are used to them, but the rest of the state may not be. Though they can be eaten fresh, most are used for jelly, cobbler, tasty juice, and occasionally wine. The way to eat a muscadine is to squeeze the juicy pulp from the middle into your mouth and discard the tough, somewhat astringent skin. The seeds are then spit at your nearest neighbor. Muscadines thrive in the humid eastern part of the state where wine and table grapes succumb to deadly Pierce's disease and fruit rot.

When to Plant

Muscadines are mostly grown in containers and can be planted any time of the year when moisture is available. As with all container-grown plants, fall planting is best, followed by winter, spring, and finally summer, which can be stressful due to heat and drought. Be aware that most nurseries and garden centers stock their fruiting plants during the late winter and early spring.

Where to Plant

Muscadines produce best in full sun with at least eight hours of direct light each day. They will tolerate most soil types as long as they are well drained, but they produce best in deep, sandy loam soil. Mucadines prefer acid soils but can tolerate those that are slightly alkaline.

How to Plant

Dig a hole the same depth but a little wider than the pot, place the rootball into it, and backfill with your existing soil. Water well. Put 1 to 2 inches of mulch (compost, pine bark, straw, and so forth) in a 3- to 4-foot circle around the plants to prevent weeds, moderate soil temperatures, and conserve moisture.

Care and Maintenance

Muscadines are generally easier to grow than grapes. Unlike most grapes, they thrive in areas of high rainfall and humidity and are not plagued with black rot or the deadly Pierce's disease. They require little to no fertilizer. If the vines are weak or you have deep, sandy soil, apply ¼ pound of a complete lawn and garden fertilizer during late winter. Like grapes, pruning and training are the biggest chores in muscadine growing. Visit your county extension agent for complete instructions on the different styles of muscadine pruning. Do not prune at all the first year. You will need to train them onto a sturdy fence, trellis, or other structure. Muscadines also produce on old wood and have a tendency to overproduce. Therefore, you must prune them heavily each year, removing about 80 percent of the vines during the winter.

Harvest

Muscadines are harvested when they are fully plump and ripe, generally during the late summer and fall. The fruit will be slightly soft and dull colored when it's ready. Eat, prepare, or refrigerate immediately.

Additional Information

Many muscadine varieties are not self-fertile (female) and must be planted with a self-fertile variety for cross-pollination. Recommended varieties for Texas include 'Carlos' (bronze, self-fertile), 'Cowart' (black, self-fertile), 'Darlene' (bronze, female), 'Florida Fry' (bronze, self-fertile), 'Fry' (bronze, female), 'Higgins' (black bronze, female), 'Hunt' (black, female), 'Ison' (black, self-fertile), 'Janebell' (bronze, self-fertile), 'Jumbo' (black, female), 'Magnolia' (bronze, self-fertile), 'Noble' (red, self-fertile), 'Pam' (bronze, female), 'Scuppernong' (bronze, female), 'Summit' (bronze, female), 'Sweet Jenny' (bronze, female), and 'Triumph' (bronze, self-fertile). Bronze muscadines are my favorites and are also known as scuppernongs. Muscadines are native to the United States and are loved by many forms of wildlife.

PEACH

The Texas Hill Country and East Texas are known for producing mouth-watering peaches (*Prunus persica*). Unfortunately, they are a bit troublesome to grow. Peaches are prone to insects and diseases, and the trees they grow on are short-lived in Texas. Producing them at home isn't impossible. You just have to be able to follow instructions and be dedicated to the cause. If you want to produce them organically, you'll have to be extra diligent. Peaches can be either white-fleshed or yellow-fleshed and either cling (the flesh sticks to the seed) or freestone (the flesh comes away from the seed easily). I like cling peaches, but most people prefer canning or cooking with freestone varieties.

When to Plant

Peach trees are generally planted during the winter or early spring. They are available as both bare-root and containerized plants. If you are planting bare-root peaches, it is absolutely a must that you plant them when they are dormant (leafless) during the winter. Containerized plants can be planted year-round, with fall being the best time, winter second, spring third, and summer the worst. Peach trees should be spaced about 15 to 20 feet apart.

Where to Plant

Peaches require full sun of at least eight hours a day (preferably more) to produce well. They can be grown in most soils but prefer well-drained, sandy loam. The ideal soil pH for peaches is between 6.0 to 6.5.

How to Plant

Dig a hole twice as wide as the tree's rootball and as deep as the roots or pot it was in. Water the rootball in the hole and then backfill the lower three-fourths of the hole with the native soil and the upper one-fourth with a mixture of the native soil and compost. Be sure not to plant the tree too deep or it will die. It's better to plant it a little high than too low. Create a circular berm around the tree that acts as a catch basin for water, and water the tree once a week until it's established. Then make sure it gets approximately 1 to 2 inches of water per week either through rainfall or irrigation.

Care and Maintenance

When your peach tree is young and developing, you will want to shape it into an open bowl shape. This will include removing the centermost branch or central leader and any overly vigorous suckers or water sprouts. This open-centered shape will let light and air in to help ripen the fruit and reduce diseases. For the first two years of the tree's life, give them a 1-pound application of a complete lawn or garden fertilizer (15-5-10, 13-13-13, and so forth) in May, June, and July each year. Mature trees should receive 1 pound of a complete fertilizer for each inch of trunk's diameter (measured at the ground) each February. Peaches are susceptible to many insects and diseases, and they must be sprayed regularly to control these.

Harvest

Peaches do not ripen off the tree and must be left on until they're fully plump, colored, and slightly soft for maximum sweetness and flavor.

Additional Information

Recommended varieties for Texas include 'Bicentennial' (cling), 'Dixieland' (freestone), 'Dixiered' (cling), 'Frank' (cling), 'Harvester' (freestone), 'Indian Cling' (cling), 'June Gold' (cling), 'Loring' (freestone), 'Ranger' (freestone), 'Redglobe' (freestone), 'Redhaven' (semi-freestone), 'Redskin' (freestone), 'Sam Houston' (freestone), and 'Sentinel' (semi-freestone). Peaches originated in China and were cultivated by American Indians after being introduced by early Spanish settlers.

PEAR

One of many ways to tell who was raised in Texas and who moved in from the North is by their response to the hard canning pears (*Pyrus pyrifolia*) that grow successfully here. If they greedily devour the hard gritty pears like free apples, then they're from Texas. If they spit them out and ask for the nearest grocery store selling 'Bartlett' pears from Washington State, then they probably moved in. Unfortunately, thanks to a devastating disease known as fire blight that kills the trees deader than a hammer, we can't grow soft, mellow European-type pears, like 'Bartlett'. Occasionally, a Texas gardener gets by with it for a few years but fire blight eventually swoops in for the kill. We can cheat by holding our pears well into the fall before eating them, which allows them to soften up considerably. These pears are famous for pear preserves, however. And my grandmother once made me a pear pie that was divine.

When to Plant

Pear trees are generally planted during the winter or early spring. They are available as both bare-root and containerized plants. If you are planting bare-root pears, it is absolutely a must that you plant them when they are

dormant (leafless) during the winter. Containerized plants can be planted year-round, with fall being the best time, winter second best, spring third best, and summer the worst. Pears should be spaced about 25 feet apart.

Where to Plant

Pears require full sun of at least eight hours a day (preferably more) to produce well. They can be grown in most any soils but prefer those that are well drained. They will tolerate both acid and alkaline soils.

How to Plant

Dig a hole twice as wide as the tree's rootball and as deep as the roots or pot it was in. Water the rootball in the hole and then backfill the hole with the native soil. Be sure not to plant the tree too deep or it will die. Create a circular berm around the tree that acts as a catch basin for water, and water the tree once a week until it's established.

Care and Maintenance

Pears require relatively little care, pruning, spraying, or fertilizing. They can be grown organically in Texas. The main problem for pears is a bacterial disease called fire blight that causes the branches to die. It is extremely important to plant only blight-resistant, hard pears in Texas.

Harvest

Pears should be fully sized and colored before picking. They will ripen off the tree and can be ripened at room temperature. To allow them to soften, wrap them individually in paper for one week to one month.

Additional Information

Pears are not self-fertile and need another variety for cross-pollination. Recommended varieties for Texas include 'Ayers', 'Garber', 'Fan-Stil', 'Kieffer', 'LeConte', 'Magness', 'Monterrey', 'Moonglow', 'Orient', and 'Warren'. Our type of pear originated in China. They are long-lived trees and can be found at many old home sites.

PERSIMMON

Asian persimmons (*Diospyros kaki*) are eye-popping small ornamental trees. They have wonderful yellow and orange fall colors and produce copious quantities of large orange fruit that hang on the tree until winter. Many nongardeners refer to them as tomato trees. Though not common here, they have been cultivated in Texas for over a hundred years and in the Orient for thousands of years. They can be eaten fresh or dried, or made into breads, cakes, and puddings. Luckily, they are very easy to grow and can be produced completely organically with almost no insect or disease problems. Though many astringent types will pucker your mouth before they are completely soft and ripe, the non-astringent types can be eaten when they are crisp and firm, like an apple. Those are my favorites.

When to Plant

Asian persimmons are generally planted during the winter or early spring. They are available as both bare-root and containerized plants. When planting bare-root persimmons, it is absolutely a must that you plant them when they are dormant (leafless) during the winter. Containerized plants can be planted year-round, as long as moisture is available, with fall being the best time, winter second, spring third, and summer the worst. Asian persimmons should be spaced 10 to 20 feet apart.

Where to Plant

Asian persimmons require full sun of at least eight hours a day to produce well. They can be grown in most any soils but prefer those that are well drained. Asian persimmons can grow in acid or moderately alkaline soils.

How to Plant

Dig a hole twice as wide as the tree's rootball and as deep as the roots or pot it was in. Water the rootball in the hole and then backfill the hole with the native soil. Be careful not to plant the tree too deep or it will die. Create a circular berm around the tree that acts as a catch basin for water, and water the tree once a week until it's established.

Care and Maintenance

Asian persimmons require relatively little care, pruning, spraying, or fertilizing. They can be grown organically in Texas. Provide 1 to 2 inches of water per week when they are in fruit to prevent fruit drop.

Harvest

Although they will ripen off the tree, persimmons should be left on the tree until they are fullsized, soft, and fully colored, generally around the first frost. If they are not ripe, they will be very astringent and pucker your mouth. Fuyu can be harvested when it is firm and crisp, as it is a non-astringent variety. Persimmons generally stay edible and hang on the tree until midwinter.

Additional Information

Persimmons are self fruitful; however fruit set and retention is often better when cross-pollinated by another variety. Seedless fruit can only occur without cross-pollination or by only having a single variety. Recommended varieties for Texas include 'Eureka', 'Fuyu' (seedless, non-astringent), 'Hachiya' (seedless), 'Tamopan', and 'Tane-nashi' (seedless). 'Fuyu' is my favorite and can be eaten when it's still firm. Asian persimmons originated in Asia.

PLUM

Plums (*Prunus salicina*) are tasty and, though not foolproof, are easier to grow and produce than peaches. They do have their own insect and disease problems, but overall they live longer and produce more than their peach cousins. They are great for fresh eating and, of course, make fabulous jelly. I loved picking and eating wild Chickasaw plums as a kid and still look for native thickets of them today. If you are lucky enough to pick a bucket full, my mom will make us some jelly. Unlike pears and hawthorns, the delicate white spring flowers of plums are sweet scented.

When to Plant

Plum trees are generally planted during the winter or early spring. They are available as both bare-root and containerized plants. If you are planting bare-root plums, it is absolutely a must that you plant them when they are dormant (leafless) during the winter. Containerized plants can be planted year-round, as long as there is moisture, with fall being the best time, winter second, spring third, and summer the worst. Plums should be spaced about 15 to 20 feet apart.

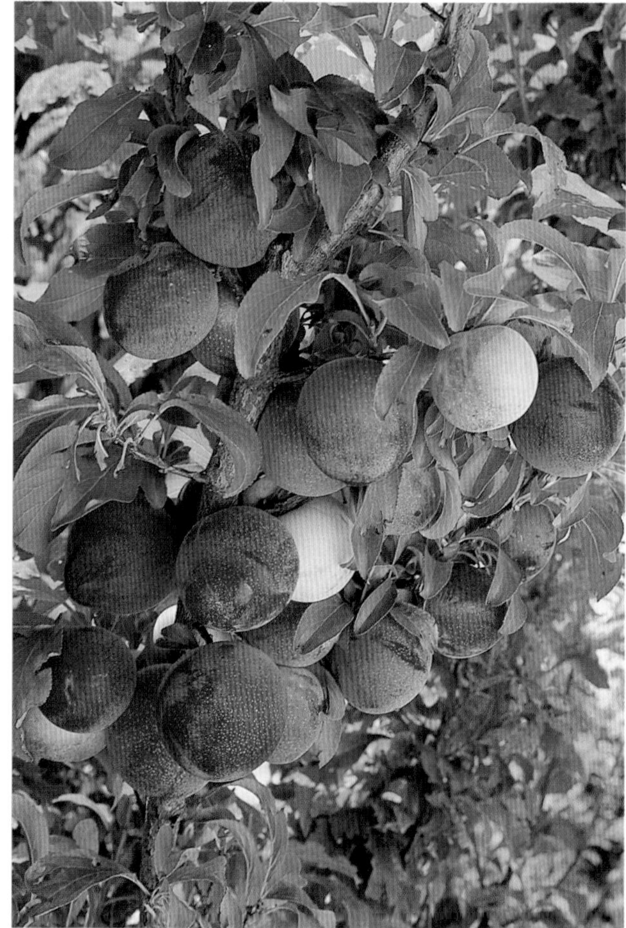

Where to Plant

Plums require full sun of at least eight hours a day (preferably more) to produce well. They can be grown in most soils but prefer well-drained, sandy loam. The ideal soil pH for plums is between 6.0 to 6.5.

How to Plant

Dig a hole twice as wide as the tree's rootball and as deep as the roots or pot it was in. Water the rootball in the hole and then backfill the lower three-fourths of the hole with the native soil and the upper one-fourth with a mixture of the native soil and compost. Do not to plant the tree too deep or it will die. It's better to plant it a little high than too low. Create a circular berm around the tree that acts as a catch basin for water, and water the tree once a week until it's established.

Care and Maintenance

When your plum trees are young and developing, you will want to shape them into an open bowl shape. This will include removing the centermost branch or central leader and any overly vigorous suckers or water sprouts. This open-centered shape will let light and air in to help ripen the fruit and reduce diseases. For the first two years of the trees' lives, apply a 1-pound application of a complete lawn or garden fertilizer (15-5-10, 13-13-13, and so forth) in May, June, and July each year. Mature trees should receive 1 pound of a complete fertilizer for each inch of trunk diameter (measured at the ground) each February. Plums are susceptible to many insects and diseases and must be sprayed regularly to control them.

Harvest

Plums will ripen after picking, but for best flavor and sweetness they should be left on the tree until fully sized and colored. You may have to purchase bird netting to keep from sharing with your neighborhood wildlife.

Additional Information

Most plums (except 'Methley') need another variety as a pollinator. Recommended plum varieties for Texas include 'Allred', 'Bruce', 'Methley' (self-fruitful, good pollinator), 'Morris', 'Ozark Premier', and 'Santa Rosa'. These plum types originated in Japan.

POMEGRANATE

One of my many sins as a young boy was annually plotting to sneak into Marie Daly's yard to snitch a luscious pomegranate (*Punica granatum*). All the neighborhood kids thought she was a *witch* and were scared to death of her, but the word was out that she had pomegranates and chinquapins in her yard. I'm not sure that I ever even got one of her pomegranates, but it wasn't because I didn't want one. She later turned out to be one of my dearest, sweetest friends on earth and would have given me all the pomegranates she owned. And now that I grow my own I can't help but think about her. Pomegranates are pretty, tough, drought-tolerant, deciduous shrubs and can be grown organically, as they don't have any insect or disease problems to speak of. The sweet-tart juice they produce is loaded with antioxidants and I can never get enough. They are a very popular fruit these days and make excellent ornamentals for hot, dry climates.

When to Plant

Pomegranates are generally grown in containers and can be planted any time of the year when moisture is available. Since pomegranates can be a bit cold tender, spring planting, after all danger of freezing has past, is recommended. Pomegranates should be spaced 8 to 10 feet apart.

Where to Plant

Pomegranates require full sun of at least eight hours a day (preferably more) for maximum production. They can be grown in most soils but prefer those that are well drained. They are tolerant of both acid and alkaline soils.

How to Plant

Dig a hole the same depth but a little wider than the pot, place the rootball into it, and backfill with your existing soil. Water well. Put 1 to 2 inches of mulch (compost, pine bark, straw, and so forth) in a 3- to 4-foot circle around the plants to prevent weeds, moderate soil temperatures, and conserve moisture.

Care and Maintenance

Pomegranates require almost no pruning, spraying, or fertilizing and can be grown organically in Texas. They mainly require sunny conditions and long, hot summers. The fruit may split in areas of high rainfall and, of course, you may have to guard them from neighborhood boys.

Harvest

Pomegranates are ripe when they are full sized, plump with seeds, and blushed with red. Eat, prepare, or refrigerate immediately. To eat a pomegranate, score around the entire skin of the fruit with a paring knife and pop it in half. Shell out the fleshy seeds into a bowl, after removing the inner white membranes, and eat them with a spoon. After extracting the juice, I spit the seeds out when no one is looking. I was eating a pomegranate when Elvis died!

Additional Information

Pomegranates are self-fruitful and do not require a pollinator. Recommended pomegranate varieties for Texas include 'Aperoski', 'Cloud', 'Kandahar Early', 'Russian #8', 'Russian #18', 'Salavatski', 'Sirenevyi', 'Surh-anor', and 'Texas Pink'. Pomegranates originated in the Middle East, are ancient symbols of fertility, and are mentioned in the Bible. The crown that kings wear was fashioned after the calyx lobes from a pomegranate fruit. Double-flowered, ornamental pomegranates usually do not set any fruit. Fruiting varieties have single flowers.

STRAWBERRY

Is there anybody on the planet that doesn't love a luscious ripe strawberry (*Fragaria virginiana*)? And don't we all wish we grew them in our backyards? Well it's very possible, if and only if, you can follow exact instructions. Strawberry production in Texas is dependent on planting transplants in the fall. Unfortunately, most nurseries and garden centers don't stock them until the spring. If you insist on planting them in the spring, plan on going to the grocery store and buying cartons of giant tasteless strawberries from California. Otherwise do what you are told, order and plant transplants in the fall, and harvest ripe tasty strawberries when everybody else is wasting their time planting theirs.

When to Plant

To grow strawberries successfully in Texas, you must plant transplants of June-bearing varieties in the fall. This allows them to get rooted when there is cool weather and moisture and form flowers before spring arrives. Plants planted in the spring succumb to heat, drought, and diseases and produce little fruit. Strawberry plants should be planted 12 inches apart.

Where to Plant

Strawberries require at least eight hours (preferably more) of direct sun each day. They need well-drained, sandy loam soil to prosper. If you have clay or poor drainage, you will need to plant them in a raised bed composed of half sand, half sphagnum peat moss or compost, and half topsoil. Apply 2 teaspoons of a complete garden fertilizer (13-13-13, 10-20-10, and so forth) per square foot or foot of row. Strawberries prefer a pH between 6.0 and 7.0.

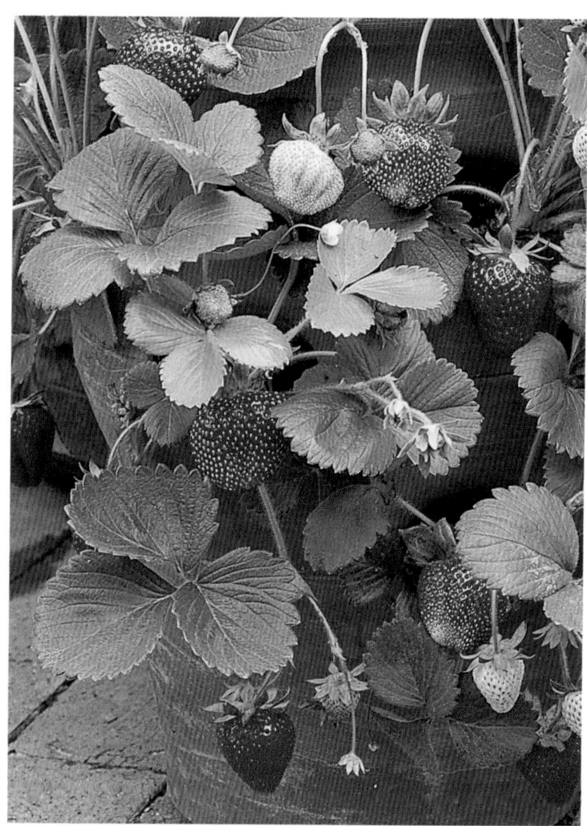

How to Plant

Strawberries need well-prepared soil. It is very critical that strawberry transplants not be planted too deep. Using a hand spade, scoop out a hole and place the bare-root transplant in it so that the roots will be below the soil and the foliage above the soil. Half of the crown (stem just above the roots) should be below the soil and half should be above the soil. Water well.

Care and Maintenance

Mulch your strawberries with hay, straw, compost, or grass clippings to prevent weeds and to keep the fruit off the ground. Side-dress the plants with an additional 2 teaspoons of complete garden fertilizer (13-13-13, 10-20-10, and so forth) per square foot or foot of row when they start to set green fruit. It's important that strawberries don't dry out so apply the equivalent of 1 to 2 inches of water per week. Your biggest enemies will be pill bugs, birds, and your neighbors. Bird netting will probably be essential. After your fall-planted strawberries produce fruit, pull them up and discard them. This prevents diseases from building up in plant material and soil. Plant new plants each fall.

Harvest

To be tasty and sweet, strawberries must ripen on the plant. Pick when fully sized and colored, and refrigerate (or eat) immediately.

Additional Information

Recommended strawberry varieties for Texas include 'Chandler', 'Camarosa', and 'Sweet Charlie'. There are three categories of strawberry varieties: June-bearing, everbearing, and day-neutral. Those that do best for us as fall-planted transplants are June (spring) bearers. Strawberries originated in North and South America.

NUTS

Short of my family, friends, and all politicians, Texas is short on nuts. I wish I could tell you how to grow Brazil nuts, cashews, English walnuts, filberts, macadamias, and pistachios, but I can't. We have to play the hand we're dealt. If you are in the eastern part of the state you have a few extra options like black walnuts, chinquapins, Chinese chestnuts, and hickory nuts, but for most of the state, you are limited to peanuts (if you have sandy soil) and of course our state tree, the pecan.

Nuts are a healthy, nutritious addition to your diet. In addition to healthy oils and fiber, nuts are high in protein like meat and eggs. Nuts were an important part of the diet of native Texas Indians and should be yours as well.

PEANUT

Peanuts (*Arachis hypogaea*), or goobers, have always been popular in Texas and the South. My family ate lots of them and still does. My dad keeps them parched on top of the wood stove and dives into them constantly. And mom still makes plenty of peanut brittle for family and friends alike to munch on. And one of our historic favorites is syrup candy that my grandmother always made us out of ribbon cane syrup, butter, and peanuts. It's somewhere between taffy and syrup, and we all still fight over it with our big spoons. I remember the first time I grew peanuts as a kid—how amazed I was that the little shoots that make peanuts start out above the ground and take a dive into the dirt. I also remember how angry I was when I hung them on the fence to dry only to have a pesky squirrel eat them all. My grandmother was also good at making squirrel dumplings.

When to Plant

Peanuts are a warm-season crop; therefore, the seed must be planted after all danger of frost in the spring, generally March in the southern half of Texas and April or later in the northern half. They cannot tolerate frost or freezing temperatures. Thin the plants to 6 to 8 inches apart.

Where to Plant

Peanuts require at least eight hours of direct sun each day for maximum yields. They do best in well-drained sandy and sandy loam soils. Ideally, till in several inches of compost or organic matter and incorporate 2 pounds of a complete garden fertilizer (10-20-10, 13-13-13, and so forth) per 100 square feet of bed or every 35 feet of row before planting. The ideal soil pH for peanuts is 6.0 to 7.0.

How to Plant

Open a shallow trench in your raised row 1 to 1½ inches deep with the corner of a hoe or a stick. Shell the peanuts and then sow the seeds four to five per foot to ensure a good stand and cover with 1 inch of soil. After seeding, gently tamp down the soil with the back of your hoe to ensure good seed-to-soil contact. Water gently and carefully, and keep the soil moist until germination occurs.

Care and Maintenance

Peanuts have few insect and disease problems. Control weeds with shallow cultivation and mulch so as not to disturb the developing nuts.

Harvest

Harvest your peanuts when the foliage begins to yellow, generally late summer or early fall. Carefully dig up the plants with a spading fork, shake the soil from them, and hang them in a warm, dry shed or barn. After they dry for several weeks, pull off the peanuts and allow them to dry several more weeks in baskets or mesh bags. Be *very* wary of mice and squirrels, as they will eagerly devour your bounty. After drying, store them in a cool, well-ventilated place until you're ready to prepare or eat them.

Additional Information

Recommended peanut varieties for Texas include 'Early Spanish', 'Jumbo Virginia', 'Virginia Improved', and 'Spanish'. Peanuts are native to South America. The name goober is from Africa. My childhood idol, George Washington Carver, was famous for his peanut promotion, inventions, and recipes.

PECAN

Everybody in Texas loves pecans (*Carya illinoinensis*). It's a law, I think. After all, it is our state tree. Don't ask me what nut gave it a botanical name honoring *Illinois* because I don't know. It should have been named for Texas, Louisiana, or Mississippi, where they are most common in the wild, and grow in profusion along rivers, in deep soils. Texas generally leads the nation in native pecan production. And all good cooks and candy makers will tell you that the small oily native pecans taste the best. One of the best days of my life was when I stumbled across the Seguin Pecans Growers Association booth at the Texas Folklife Festival years ago in San Antonio. They were selling chewy pecans pralines and handing out the recipe as well. They were the most heavenly things I'd ever eaten and we've made them, fought over them, and hoarded them every Christmas since. Two cartons of cream, a pound of butter, and 8 cups of pecans is worth fighting for.

When to Plant

Pecan trees are generally planted during the winter or early spring. They are available as both bare-root and containerized plants. If you are planting

bare-root pecans, it is absolutely a must that you plant them when they are dormant during the winter. Containerized plants can be planted year-round, as long as there is moisture, with fall being the best time, winter second, spring third, and summer the worst. Pecans should be spaced about 50 feet apart.

Pollination

Pecans require cross-pollination with another variety to make nuts. Pecan varieties are divided into two categories. Some make their male flowers (shed their pollen) first while the others make their female flowers (future pecans) first. Each type naturally pollinates the other. It's critical that you plant at least one variety from each category or have existing native pecans nearby. Pecans are wind pollinated and can cross-pollinate up to ¼ of a mile away. However, for consistent pollination, you'll want to make sure your tree is within 300 feet of an appropriate pollinator variety, native tree, or other seedling tree.

PECAN POLLINATOR VARIETIES*

Male (pollen first)	Female (nutlets first)
Caddo	Choctaw
Cape Fear	Elliot
Cheyenne	Kiowa
Desirable	Mohawk
Pawnee	Shawnee
Western	Shoshoni Sioux Wichita

*Plant at least one variety from each category to insure good cross-pollination.

Where to Plant

Pecan trees require at least eight hours of direct sun (preferably more) for maximum production. They will grow in most soils but produce best in those that are deep, fertile, and well drained.

How to Plant

Dig a hole twice as wide as the tree's rootball and as deep as the roots or pot it was in. Water the rootball in the hole and then backfill with the native soil. Make sure not to plant the tree too deep or it will die. Create a circular berm around the tree that acts as a catch basin for water and water the tree once a week until it's established. Keep a 4-inch deep and 4-foot wide ring of mulch (compost, bark, hay, and so forth) around the base of the tree until it exceeds 6 inches in diameter. This mulch will help conserve moisture and keep the soil cooler during the summer, warmer during the winter, and keep nearby weeds and grass from stunting the growth of the tree. Remember that tree roots and grass roots all grow in the same area of soil where oxygen is available. This ring of mulch will also keep lawn mowers and string trimmers from damaging the bark of the tree. Any damage to the trunk will not only limit the growth of the tree but can lead to a borer invasion and possible death.

Care and Maintenance

From the time your pecan tree is young, you will want to start training it to have a main central leader with side branches coming off of it at wide angles. During the first two or three growing seasons, growth should be continually forced into the central leader by "pinching" or cutting back the lateral or side shoots as they develop. As with all trees, if two central leaders (main trunks) develop, be sure to remove one, otherwise the tree is almost guaranteed to split apart later in life. By creating a tree with a strong central leader and wide-angled side branches, you will minimize limb breakage when the tree produces heavy crops later. Pecans respond well to fertilizer, and starting in the second year they should receive 1 pound of a high-nitrogen fertilizer (15-5-10, 21-0-0, and so forth) in April, May, and June. After the trees reach 6 inches in diameter, give them 1 pound for each inch of trunk diameter, sprinkled uniformly under the drip line (outside edge of branches) of the tree. Make sure they receive 1 to 2 inches of water per week, especially when the nuts are on the tree.

Pecan Pests

Pecans have a host of potential insect and disease problems, including aphids, phylloxera gall, pecan nut casebearer, scab, and fall webworms. Visit your county extension agent for their latest prevention and control methods.

Aphids are very small insects that feed on pecan foliage, as well as many other plants. They can be easily recognized by the sticky film of "honeydew" (sugar water excretion) that accumulates on the surface of the leaves and anything below the trees. Generally a black, harmless, fungus known as sooty mold grows on the honeydew for its own nourishment.

Phylloxera galls are caused by a small piercing-sucking insect that inject a toxin into the new growth in the spring, forming small, round, green galls on the pecan twigs and leaves from April to June.

Pecan nut casebearer is a small insect, which feeds on the nut and causes it to fall from the tree prematurely. The damage is easily noticed as the insect always enters the pecan on the stem end of the fruit. A generation usually appears in early May, followed by a second generation 42 days later.

Scab is the most common pecan disease in the South. It is most severe in areas with high rain fall, like East Texas and the Gulf Coast.This fungus causes black spots on the leaves and pecan shucks in early spring and may cause the entire shuck to turn black.

Fall webworms create thick webs or tents around their clustered populations in August, September, and October and can eat every leaf on a tree. On small trees, the webs, along with the caterpillars, can be pruned from the tree and destroyed.

Harvest

Pecans ripen in the fall and will fall to the ground when ripe. Allow them to dry several more weeks in a well-ventilated area and then store in the refrigerator or freezer.

Additional Information

Pecans are not self-fertile and require two compatible varieties for cross-pollination. See your county extension agent for a list of compatible varieties. Recommended pecan varieties for Texas include 'Caddo', 'Cape Fear', 'Cheyenne', 'Choctaw', 'Desirable', 'Forkert', 'Houma', 'Kiowa', 'Oconee', 'Pawnee' (West Texas only), 'Sioux' (West Texas only), and 'Wichita' (West Texas only). Pecans are native to the United States.

NEED MORE HELP?

Please promise me you won't give up after your first few failures. Producing edible crops is a huge gamble. We can easily control variety selection and fertility, but we can't always control the amount of water our plants get, and we can *never* control the weather. Even with the most experienced gardener or professional farmer, there are disasters and crop failures. The key is to figure out what went wrong and move on to the next crop.

I've been gardening for nearly fifty years now, received degrees in both floriculture and horticulture, worked for all three branches of the land grant university system

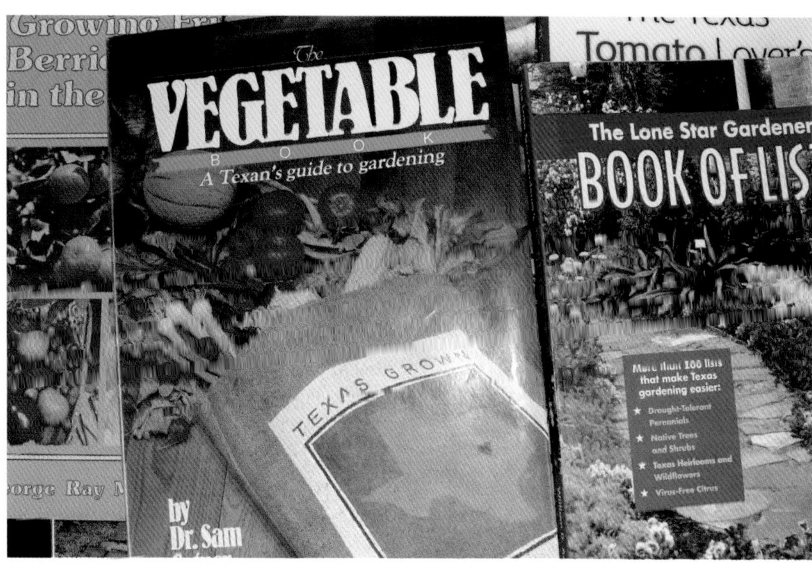

(teaching, research, and extension), but I still experience crop disasters and puzzling problems like all other Texas gardeners. It's the nature of the beast. You will never learn all that you need to know. But to get better, you need to keep learning all the time. Visit every Southern garden that you can. Read every Texas gardening book and magazine that you can. And attend every Texas gardening lecture, class, or seminar that you can. Learning about gardening in Texas is like picking a mess of peas. You do it one pod at a time. If you want lots of peas, you have to pick lots of peas. There's no easy, lazy way to do it. Learning about our number one hobby is an enjoyable experience. Here's some additional information to send you farther down the row.

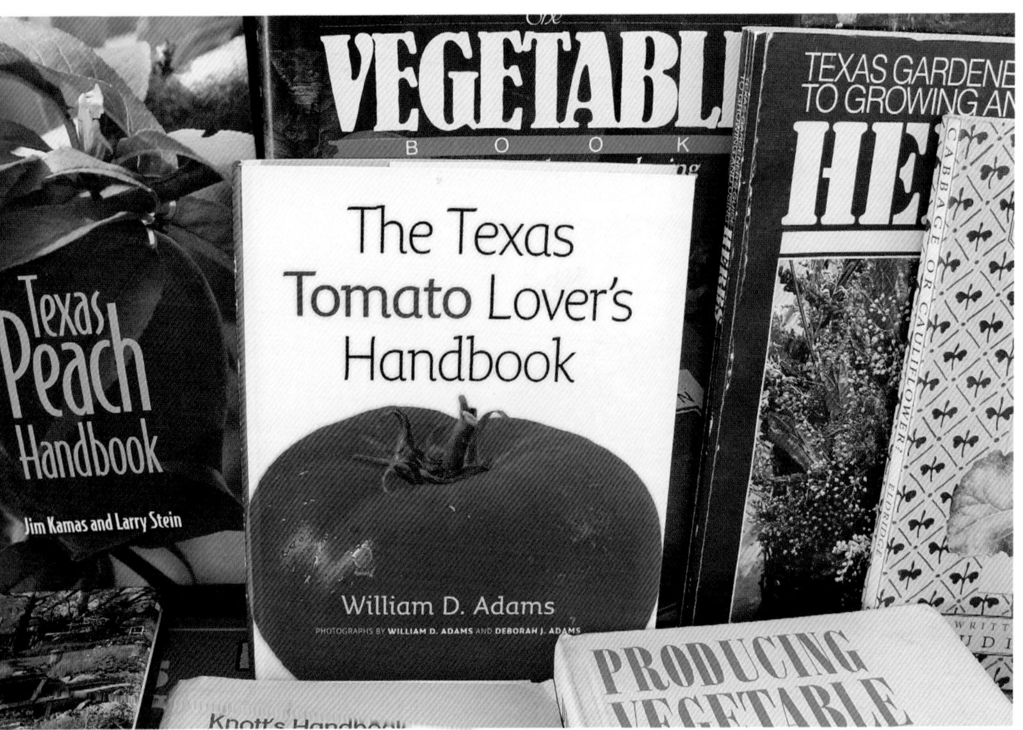

COMMON ORGANIC FERTILIZERS

Fertilizer	% Nitrogen (N)	% Phosphorus (P)	% Potassium (K)
Blood	10	1.5	0
Fish scraps	9	7	0
Guano (bat)	6	9	3
Guano (bird)	13	11	3
Kelp (seaweed)	1	0.5	9
Meal (bone-raw)	4	22	0
Meal (bone-steamed)	2	27	0
Meal (cocoa shell)	2.5	1	3
Meal (cotton seed)	6	2.5	2
Meal (hoof and horn)	14	0	0
Manure (cattle)	0.5	0.3	0.5
Manure (chicken)	0.9	0.5	0.8
Manure (horse)	0.6	0.3	0.6
Manure (pig)	0.6	0.5	0.4
Manure (sheep)	0.9	0.5	0.8
Mushroom compost	1	1	1
Oyster shells	0.2	0.3	0
Peat (muck)	2	0.3	0.3
Rice hulls (ground)	0.5	0.2	0.5
Sewage sludge	2	1	1
Sewage sludge (activated)	6	5	0
Tankage (cocoa)	4	1.5	2
Tankage (garbage)	3	3	1
Tankage (leather, hair, wool, felt, feathers)	8	2	0
Wood ashes	0	2	6

LAST & FIRST FREEZE DATES

City	Last Spring Freeze	First Fall Freeze
Abilene	March 26	November 12
Alice	February 20	December 4
Alpine	March 30	November 10
Amarillo	April 20	October 28
Angleton	March 2	November 30
Austin	March 7	November 22
Ballinger	March 30	November 10
Beaumont	February 18	November 24
Beeville	February 20	December 5
Big Spring	March 29	November 11
Boerne	March 25	November 9
Bonham	March 30	November 7
Borger	April 17	October 28
Brenham	February 25	December 2
Bridgeport	March 30	November 5
Bronson	March 24	November 8
Brownsville	January 10	*
Brownwood	March 20	November 18
Cameron	March 15	November 21
Canadian	April 9	October 30
Carrizo Springs	February 22	November 26
Center	March 17	November 6
Centerville	March 14	November 9
Childress	April 1	November 7
Clarksville	March 26	November 5
Cleburne	March 26	November 10
Coleman	March 28	November 5
College Station	March 6	November 27
Colorado City	April 5	November 3
Conroe	March 6	November 23

LAST & FIRST FREEZE DATES

City	Last Spring Freeze	First Fall Freeze
Corpus Christi	February 9	December 12
Corsicana	March 13	November 20
Crockett	March 16	November 9
Crosbyton	April 11	November 2
Crystal City	March 2	November 27
Cuero	March 8	November 27
Dalhart	April 25	October 16
Dallas	March 18	November 12
Danevang	February 23	December 5
Del Rio	February 10	December 10
Denison Dam	March 26	November 10
Dilley	February 25	December 2
Dublin	March 26	November 17
Eagle Pass	February 20	December 3
Eastland	March 29	November 9
Eden	April 3	November 7
El Campo	February 27	December 2
El Paso	March 14	November 12
Falfurrias	February 10	December 10
Flatonia	March 4	December 4
Follet	April 20	October 28
Fort Stockton	April 2	November 10
Fort Worth	March 20	November 15
Fredericksburg	March 27	November 3
Gainesville	March 29	November 6
Galveston	January 25	December 23
Gatesville	March 24	November 9
Goliad	February 22	December 1
Graham	April 3	November 2
Greenville	March 20	November 12

LAST & FIRST FREEZE DATES

City	Last Spring Freeze	First Fall Freeze
Hallettsville	March 8	November 15
Harlingen	January 24	December 26
Henderson	March 11	November 13
Hereford	April 23	October 24
Hico	March 29	November 2
Hondo	March 3	November 21
Houston	February 4	December 10
Hunstville	March 9	November 27
Iowa Park	April 1	November 2
Jacksboro	April 2	November 2
Junction	April 2	November 2
Karnack	March 18	November 4
Kaufman	March 21	November 15
Kenedy	March 5	November 26
Kerrville	April 4	November 6
Kirbyville	March 22	November 7
Knox City	April 1	November 9
Laredo	January 1	December 19
Levelland	April 13	October 30
Liberty	March 1	November 15
Lindale	March 12	November 11
Livingston	March 14	November 17
Llano	March 27	November 10
Longview	March 15	November 12
Lubbock	April 11	November 1
Lufkin	March 18	November 4
Luling	March 3	November 24
Madisonville	March 9	November 12
Marathon	April 5	November 1
Marshall	March 14	November 13

LAST & FIRST FREEZE DATES

City	Last Spring Freeze	First Fall Freeze
Matagorda	February 13	December 14
Maurbo	February 23	December 2
McAllen	January 30	December 10
McCook	February 5	December 8
McKinney	April 1	November 5
Mexia	March 16	November 21
Midland	April 2	November 6
Mineral Wells	March 25	November 6
Mission	January 26	December 18
Montague	March 29	November 6
Mount Locke	April 23	October 26
Mount Pleasant	March 25	November 9
Muleshoe	April 20	October 20
Nacogdoches	March 16	November 10
New Braunfels	March 11	November 26
Palacios	February 12	December 4
Palestine	March 14	November 15
Paris	March 27	November 10
Pecos	March 31	November 8
Pierce	March 6	November 27
Plainview	April 11	November 4
Port Isabel	January 9	x
Port Lavaca	February 18	December 8
Port O'Connor	February 6	December 20
Poteet	March 6	November 19
Presidio	March 18	November 13
Quanah	April 3	November 4
Raymondville	January 25	December 22
Rising Star	March 28	November 6
Roscoe	April 6	November 6

LAST & FIRST FREEZE DATES

City	Last Spring Freeze	First Fall Freeze
Rusk	March 16	November 8
San Angelo	March 25	November 13
San Antonio	March 3	November 26
San Marcos	March 13	November 19
Sealy	February 27	December 2
Seymour	April 4	October 31
Sherman	March 20	November 7
Smithville	March 11	November 15
Snyder	April 5	November 4
Spearman	April 22	October 24
Spur	April 17	October 28
Sugarland	February 14	November 29
Sulphur Springs	March 24	November 3
Tahoka	April 6	November 5
Taylor	March 14	November 18
Temple	March 10	November 24
Throckmorton	April 4	November 7
Uvalde	March 9	November 18
Van Horn	March 31	November 5
Vega	April 21	October 21
Victoria	February 6	December 8
Waco	March 16	November 18
Waxahachie	March 25	November 5
Weatherford	March 28	November 7
Weslaco	January 22	December 13
Whitney Dam	March 18	November 10
Wichita Falls	April 4	November 6
Winter Haven	February 24	December 1

* Occurs only once every decade or less.

RECOGNIZING SYMPTOMS OF NUTRIENT DEFICIENCIES

Mineral	Symptom
Nitrogen (N)	Stunted plants, yellow or light green from the bottom up and leaf tips back to the petioles. Reduced size. Slow growth. This is the most common nutritional deficiency by far.
Phosphorus (P)	Stunted plants, short internodes, purple or dark green foliage; dying old leaves; poor flowering and fruiting. Slow growth and delayed maturity.
Potassium (K)	Older leaves scorched on the margins; weak stems; fruit shriveled, uneven ripening.
Calcium (Ca)	Young leaves turn yellow and then brown; growing tip bends; weak stems; short dark roots.
Magnesium (Mg)	Thin leaves, with leaves yellow between the veins from the bottom of the plant up; tend to curve upward.
Iron (Fe)	New leaves at the top of the plant are yellow with green veins; margins and tips often stay green.
Manganese (Mn)	Tissue between the veins turns white; leaves have dead spots, plants are dwarf.
Zinc (Zn)	Terminal leaves are small; bud formation is poor; leaves have dead areas.
Boron (B)	Tip of growing plant dies; bud becomes light green; roots are brown in the center; flowers do not form.

REFRIGERATION STORAGE TIME FOR VEGETABLE SEEDS

Vegetable	Years
Asparagus	3
Bean	3
Beet	4
Broccoli	5
Brussels Sprouts	5
Cabbage	5
Cantaloupe	5
Carrot	3
Cauliflower	5
Collards	5
Corn	2
Cucumber	5
Eggplant	5
Kale	5
Lettuce	5
Mustard	4
Okra	2
Onion	2
Parsley	2
Pea, English/Snow	3
Pea, Southern	3
Pepper, Hot/Sweet	4
Pumpkin	4
Radish	5
Spinach	5
Squash, Summer/Winter	5
Swiss Chard	4
Tomato	4
Turnip	5
Watermelon	5

VEGETABLE STORAGE REQUIREMENTS

Vegetable	Ideal Temp. °F	Relative Humidity %	Average Storage Life
Asparagus	32	95	2–3 weeks
Bean (green)	40–45	90–95	7–10 days
Beet	32	95	1–3 months
Broccoli	32	90–95	10–14 days
Brussels Sprouts	32	90–95	3–5 weeks
Cabbage	32	90–95	3–4 months
Cantaloupe	32	85–90	5–14 days
Carrots	32	90–95	4–6 months
Cauliflower	32	90–95	2–4 weeks
Cucumber	45–50	90–95	10–14 days
Collards	32	90–95	10–14 days
Corn	32	90–95	4–8 days
Eggplant	45–50	90	1 week
Garlic	32	65–70	6–7 months
Kale	32	90–95	10–14 days
Lettuce	34	95	2–3 weeks
Okra	45–50	90–95	7–10 days
Onion	32	65–70	5–8 months
Peas	32	90–95	1–3 weeks
Pepper	45–50	90–95	8–10 days
Potato	38–40	90	5–8 months
Pumpkin	50–55	70–75	2–3 months
Spinach	32	90–95	10–14 days
Sweet potato	55–60	85–90	4–6 months
Tomato	45–50	85–90	4–7 days
Turnip	32	90–95	4–5 months
Radish	32	90–95	3–4 weeks
Squash (summer)	32–50	90	5–14 days
Watermelon	40–50	80–85	2–3 weeks

GROWING TRANSPLANTS 101

Vegetable	Weeks to Grow Transplant	Seed Planting Depth (inches)	Ideal Temperature for Germination	Growing Temperatures (degrees F.)
Cabbage, broccoli, cauliflower	5 to 7	¼ to ½	85	60–70 (day), 50–60 (night)
Cucumber, squash, cantaloupe, watermelon	2 to 3	¾ to 1	85	70–90 (day), 60–70 (night)
Eggplant	7 to 8	¼ to ½	85	70–80 (day), 65–70 (night)
Lettuce	4 to 6	¼ to ½	75	60–70 (day), 50–60 (night)
Onion	8 to 10	½	75	60–70 (day), 45–55 (night)
Pepper	7 to 8	¼ to ½	85	70–80 (day), 60–70 (night)

ADJUSTING SOIL pH

Pounds of Limestone (per 100 Square Feet) to Raise Your Soil pH

Change in pH Desired	Sandy Soils	Loamy Soils	Clay Soils
4.5 to 6.5	5	13.5	19.5
5.0 to 6.5	4	10.5	15.5
5.5 to 6.5	3	8	11
6.0 to 6.5	1.5	4	5.5
Above 6.0	0	0	0

Pounds of Sulphur (per 100 Square Feet) to Lower Your Soil pH

Change in pH Desired	Sandy Soils	Clay Soils
8.5 to 6.5	4.5	7
8.0 to 6.5	3	4.5
7.5 to 6.5	1	2
Less than 7.0	0	0

VEGETABLE PLANTING

Vegetable	Seed or Plants per 100 feet pl. = plants	Depth of Seed Planting in Inches	Inches of Distance Between Rows	Inches of Distance Between Plants	Average Height of Crop in Feet	Spring Planting in Regard to Average Frost-Free Date (FFD)
Asparagus	66 pl., 1 oz.	6–8, 1–1½	36–48	18	5	4 to 6 wks. before FFD
Beans, snap bush	½ lb.	1–1½	30–36	3–4	1½	on FFD to 4 wks. after
Beans, snap pole	½ lb.	1–1½	36–48	4–6	6	on FFD to 4 wks. after
Beans, Lima bush	½ lb.	1–1½	30–36	3–4	1½	on FFD to 4 wks. after
Beans, Lima pole	¼ lb.	1–1½	36–48	12–18	6	on FFD to 4 wks. after
Beets	1 oz.	1	14–24	2	1½	4 to 6 wks. before FFD
Broccoli	¼ oz.	½	24–36	14–24	3	4 to 6 wks. before FFD
Brussels Sprouts	¼ oz.	½	24–36	14–24	2	4 to 6 wks. before FFD
Cabbage	¼ oz.	½	24–36	14–24	1½	4 to 6 wks. before FFD
Cabbage, Chinese	¼ oz.	½	18–30	8–12	1½	4 to 6 wks. before FFD
Carrot	½ oz.	½	14–24	2	1	4 to 6 wks. before FFD
Cauliflower	¼ oz.	½	24–36	14–24	3	not recommended
Chard, Swiss	2 oz.	1	18–30	6	1½	2 to 6 wks. before FFD
Collard (Kale)	¼ oz.	½	18–36	6–12	2	2 to 6 wks. before FFD
Corn, sweet	3–4 oz.	1–2	24–36	9–12	6	on FFD to 6 wks. after
Cucumber	½ oz.	½	48–72	8–12	1	on FFD to 6 wks. after
Eggplant	⅛ oz.	½	30–36	18–24	3	2 to 6 wks. after FFD
Garlic	1 lb.	1–2	14–24	2–4	1	not recommended
Kohlrabi	¼ oz.	¼	14–24	4–6	1½	2 to 6 wks. before FFD

VEGETABLE PLANTING

Fall Planting in Regard to Average Autumn Freeze Date (AFD)	No. Days Ready for Use	Average Length of Harvest Season (Days)	Average Crop Expected Per 100 Feet	Approximate Planting per Person: Fresh pl. = plants	Approximate Planting per Person: (Storage) Canning or Freezing
not recommended	730	60	30 lb.	10–15 pl.	10–15 pl.
8 to 10 wks. before AFD	45–60	14	120 lb.	15–16 ft.	15–20 ft.
14 to 16 wks. before AFD	60–70	30	150 lb.	5–6 ft.	8–10 ft.
8 to 10 wks. before AFD	65–80	14	25 lb. shelled	10–15 ft.	15–20 ft.
14 to 16 wks. before AFD	75–85	40	50 lb. shelled	5–6 ft.	8–10 ft.
8 to 10 wks. before AFD	50–60	30	150 lb.	5–10 ft.	10–20 ft.
10 to 16 wks. before AFD	60–80	40	100 lb.	3–5 pl.	5–6 pl.
10 to 14 wks. before AFD	90–100	21	75 lb.	2–5 pl.	5–8 pl.
10 to 16 wks. before AFD	60–90	40	150 lb.	3–4 pl.	5–10 pl.
12 to 14 wks. before AFD	65–70	21	80 heads	3–10 ft.	—
12 to 14 wks. before AFD	70–80	21	100 lb.	5–10 ft.	10–15 ft.
10 to 16 wks. before AFD	70–90	14	100 lb.	3–5 pl.	8–12 pl.
12 to 16 wks. before AFD	45–55	40	75 lb.	3–5 pl.	8–12 pl.
8 to 12 wks. before AFD	50–80	60	100 lb.	5–10 ft.	5–10 ft.
12 to 14 wks. before AFD	70–90	10	10 doz.	10–15 ft.	30–50 ft.
10 to 12 wks. before AFD	50–70	30	120 lb.	1–2 hls.	3–5 hls.
12 to 16 wks. before AFD	80–90	90	100 lb.	2–3 pl.	2–3 pl.
4 to 6 wks. before AFD	140–150	—	40 lb.	—	1–5 ft.
12 to 16 wks. before AFD	55–75	14	75 lb.	3–5 ft.	5–10 ft.
10 to 14 wks. before AFD	40–80	21	50 lb.	5–15 ft.	—

VEGETABLE PLANTING

Vegetable	Seed or Plants per 100 feet pl. = plants	Depth of Seed Planting in Inches	Inches of Distance Between Rows	Plants	Average Height of Crop in Feet	Spring Planting in Regard to Average Frost-Free Date (FFD)
Lettuce	¼ oz.	½	18–24	2–3	1	6 wks. before FFD to 2 wks. after
Muskmelon	½ oz.	1	60–96	24–36	1	on FFD to 6 wks. after (Cantaloupe)
Mustard	¼ oz.	½	14–24	6–12	1½	on FFD to 6 wks. after
Okra	2 oz.	1	36–42	12–24	6	2 to 6 wks. after FFD
Onion (plants)	400–600 pl.	1–2	14–24	2–3	1½	4 to 10 wks. before FFD
Onion (seed)	1 oz.	½	14–24	2–3	1½	6 to 8 wks. before FFD
Peas, English	1 lb.	2–3	18–36	1	2	2 to 8 wks. before FFD
Peas, Southern	½ lb.	2–3	24–36	4–6	2½	2 to 10 wks. after FFD
Pepper	⅛ oz.	½	30–36	18–24	3	1 to 8 wks. after FFD
Potato, Irish	6–10 lb.	4	30–36	10–15	2	4 to 6 wks. before FFD
Potato, sweet	75–100 pl.	3–5	36–48	12–16	1	2 to 8 wks. after FFD
Pumpkin	½ oz.	1–2	60–96	36–48	1	1 to 4 wks. after FFD
Radish	1 oz.	½	14–24	1	½	6 wks. before FFD to 4wks. after
Spinach	1 oz.	½	14–24	3–4	1	1 to 8 wks. before FFD
Squash, summer	1 oz.	1–2	36–60	18–36	3	1 to 4 wks. after FFD
Squash, winter	½ oz.	1–2	60–96	24–48	1	1 to 4 wks. after FFD
Tomato	50 pl., ⅛ oz.	4–6, ½	36–48	36–48	3	on to 8 wks. after FFD
Turnip, greens	½ oz.	½	14–24	2–3	1½	2 to 6 wks. before FFD
Turnip, roots	½ oz.	½	14–24	2–3	1½	2 to 6 wks. before FFD
Watermelon	1 oz.	1–2	72–96	36–72	1	on FFD to 6 wks. after

Source: Texas Agricultural Extension Service

VEGETABLE PLANTING

Fall Planting in Regard to Average Autumn Freeze Date (AFD)	No. Days Ready for Use	Average Length of Harvest Season (Days)	Average Crop Expected Per 100 Feet	Approximate Planting per Person: Fresh pl. = plants	Approximate Planting per Person: (Storage) Canning or Freezing
14 to 16 wks. before AFD	85–100	30	100 fruits	3–5 hls.	—
10 to 16 wks. before AFD	30–40	30	100 lb.	5–10 ft.	10–15 ft.
12 to 16 wks. before AFD	55–65	90	100 lb.	4–6 ft.	6–10 ft.
not recommended	80–120	40	100 lb.	3–5 ft.	30–50 ft.
8 to 10 wks. before AFD	90–120	40	100 lb.	3–5 ft.	30–50 ft.
2 to 12 wks. before AFD	55–90	7	20 lb.	15–20 ft.	40–60 ft.
10 to 12 wks. before AFD	60–70	30	40 lb.	10–15 ft.	20–50 ft.
12 to 16 wks. before AFD	60–90	90	60 lb.	3–5 pl.	3–5 pl.
14 to 16 wks. before AFD	75–100	—	100 lb.	50–100 ft.	—
not recommended	100–130	—	100 lb.	5–10 pl.	10–20 pl.
12 to 14 wks. before AFD	75–100	—	100 lb.	1–2 hls.	1–2 hls.
on to 8 wks. before AFD	25–40	7	100 bunches	3–5 ft.	—
2 to 16 wks. before AFD	40–60	40	3 bu.	5–10 ft.	10–15 ft.
12 to 15 wks. before AFD	50–60	40	150 lb.	2–3 hls.	2–3 hls.
12 to 14 wks. before AFD	85–100	—	100 lb.	1–3 hls.	1–3 hls.
12 to 14 wks. before AFD	70–90	40	100 lb.	3–5 pl.	5–10 pl.
2 to 12 wks. before AFD	30	40	50–100 lb.	5–10 ft.	—
2 to 12 wks. before AFD	30–60	30	50–100 lb.	5–10 ft.	5–10 ft.
14 to 16 wks. before AFD	80–100	30	40 fruits	2–4 hls.	—

ANNUAL HERBS

Common Name *Botanical Name*	Height	Spacing Row	 Plants	Cultural Hints/Uses
Anise *Pimpinella anisum*	24 in.	18 in.	10 in.	Grow from seed. Plant after frost. Sun. Leaves for seasoning, garnish; use dried seed as spice.
Basil, Sweet *Ocimum basilicum*	20–24 in.	18 in.	12 in.	Grow from seed. Plant after frost. Sun. Season soups, stews, salad, omelets.
Borage *Borago officinalis*	24 in.	18 in.	12 in.	Grow from seed, self-sowing. Best in dry, sunny areas. Young leaves in salads and cool drinks.
Caraway *Carum carvi*	12–24 in.	18 in.	10 in.	Grow from seed. Biennial seed-bearer. Sun. Flavoring, especially bakery items.
Chervil *Anthriscus cerefolium*	10 in.	15 in.	3–6 in.	Sow in early spring. Partial shade. Aromatic leaves used in soups and salads.
Coriander *Coriandrum sativum*	24 in.	24 in.	18 in.	Grow from seed. Sow in spring, in sun or partial shade. Seed used in confections. Leaves in salad.
Dill *Anethum graveolens*	24–36 in.	24 in.	12 in.	Grow from seed sown in early spring. Sun or partial shade. Leaves and seeds used for flavoring and pickling.
Fennel (Florence Fennel) *Foeniculum vulgare*	60 in.	18 in.	18 in.	Grow from seed sown in early spring. Sun, partial shade. Has anise-like flavor for salad. Stalk eaten raw or braised.
Parsley *Petroselinum crispum*	5 in.	18 in.	6 in.	Grow from seed started in early spring. Slow to germinate. Sun. Biennial. Brings out flavor of other herbs. Fine base and seasoning.
Summer Savory *Satureja hortensis*	18 in.	18 in.	18 in.	Grow in well-worked loam. Sow seed in spring. Sun. Use leaves fresh or dry for salads, dressings, stews.

PERENNIAL HERBS

Common Name *Botanical Name*	Height	Spacing Row	Plants	Cultural Hints/Uses
Chives *Allium shoenosprusum*	12 in.	12 in.	12 in.	Little care. Divide when overcrowded. Grow from seed or by division. Favorite of chefs. Snip tops finely. Good indoor pot plant.
Hyssop *Hyssopus officinalis*	24 in.	18 in.	15 in.	Grow in poor soil, from seed. Hardy. Sun. A mint with highly aromatic, pungent leaves.
Lavender *Lavandula* spp.	24 in.	18 in.	18 in.	Grows in dry, rocky, sunny locations with plenty of lime in soil. Fresh in salads, or flowers dried for sachets, potpourri.
Oregano *Origanum vulgare*	24 in.	18 in.	9 in.	Grows in poor soil from seed or division. Sun. Flavoring for tomato dishes, pasta.
Peppermint *Mentha piperita*	36 in.	24 in.	18 in.	Can start from seed, but cuttings recommended. Sun or shade. Cut before it goes to seed. Sun. Aromatic; used as flavoring oil, used in products such as chewing gum, liqueurs, toilet water, soap, candy.
Rosemary *Rosmarinus officinalis*	3–6 ft.	18 in.	12 in.	Grows in well-drained non-acid soil. From cuttings or seed. Sun. Leaves flavor sauces, meats, and soups.
Sage *Salvia officinalis*	18 in.	24 in.	12 in.	From seed or cuttings. Full sun. Grows slow from seed. Renew bed every 3–4 years. Seasoning for meats, herb teas; used either fresh or dried.
Spearmint *Mentha spicata*	18 in.	24 in.	18 in.	Grows in moist soils. Hardy. From cuttings, divsion. Sun. Aromatic, for flavoring, condiments, teas.
Sweet Marjoram *Marjorana hortensis*	12 in.	18 ft.	12 in.	From seed or cuttings, as annual, or overwinter as potted plant. Sun. Seasoning, fresh or dried.
Tarragon *Artemisia dracunculus*	24 in.	24 in.	24 in.	Does best in semi-shade. By division or root cuttings. Protect during cold winters. European herb of aster family; aromatic seasoning.
Thyme *Thymus vulgaris*	8–12 in.	18 in.	12 in.	Grows in light, well-drained soil. Renew plants every few years. By cuttings, seed, division. Sun. Aromatic foliage for seasoning meats, soups, and dressings.

TEXAS AGRILIFE EXTENSION

One of my first jobs was as the Bexar County horticulturist in San Antonio, for what was then known as the Texas Agricultural Extension Service. It was where I first met legendary Texas vegetable specialist, teacher, entertainer, and local folk hero Dr. Jerry Parsons. It was also where I got to know what was left of the famous Belgian farmers, the Verstuyfts and the Verstraetens, in the northern part of what was known as "The Winter Garden" area of Texas. They were amazing folks and even more amazing growers. They didn't just grow vegetables—they produced vegetables. It was in their blood and it showed.

The Extension Service was a wonderful place to start my career, as I've always loved learning and as both of my parents were teachers, I've always loved teaching. The Extension Service does both. The Texas Agricultural Extension Service later changed its name to Texas AgriLife Extension, but still carries out its mission offering practical how-to education to the public based on university research. Every county in the state has a county agent whom you can contact for gardening information by calling them or visiting their office. Traditionally, most county agents specialized in "cows and plows," but today the offices offer a wide range of expertise—ranging from managing your retirement money to preparing healthy meals. Of course, they still offer recommendations on what varieties of fruits and vegetables to grow, so check them out if you haven't already. Most of their information is available online at http://agrilifeextension.tamu.edu/ or through the Texas A&M Department of Horticultural Sciences website at http://aggie-horticulture.tamu.edu.

In addition to traditional agricultural agents and family and consumer science agents, most urban areas of the state also employ county horticultural agents, or "county horticulturists," who specialize in horticulture only. If you really want to learn about horticulture, these are the guys and gals to visit. Not only was I the county horticulturist in Bexar County, I was also later the county horticulturist in Cherokee County, where the majority of the state's bedding plants are produced. Most of the counties which have county horticulturists also have Master Gardener programs that you can join. To become a certified Master Gardener, you have to complete a minimum of fifty hours of formal training through the Extension Service and contribute back fifty hours of volunteer service. Being a Master Gardener is a great way to serve your community while sharing the camaraderie and friendship of others who enjoy gaining and sharing horticultural knowledge. As far as I know, I'm the only person in Texas ever to teach a Master Gardener program and take a Master Gardener program at the same time! Not all counties have a Master Gardener program. To find out if your county offers one, contact your county Extension Service.

The counties that offer programs include the following.

- Anderson County
- Angelina County
- Aransas County
- Austin County (Bluebonnet Master Gardener Association)
- Bell County
- Bexar County
- Brazoria County
- Brazos County
- Burnet County (Highland Lakes Master Gardeners)
- Cameron County
- Cherokee County
- Collin County (Collin County Master Gardener Association)
- Coke County (Concho Valley Master Gardeners)
- Comal County
- Cooke County
- Colorado County (Bluebonnet Master Gardener Association)
- Concho County (Concho Valley Master Gardeners)
- Dallas County
- Denton County
- Ector County (Permian Basin Master Gardeners)
- El Paso County
- Ellis County
- Fannin County
- Fayette County (Bluebonnet Master Gardener Association)
- Fort Bend County
- Galveston County
- Grayson County
- Gregg County
- Grimes County
- Guadalupe County
- Harris County

- Harrison County
- Henderson County
- Hood County (Lake Granbury Master Gardeners)
- Howard County
- Hunt County
- Jasper County
- Johnson County
- Kaufman County
- Kerr County (Hill County Master Gardeners)
- Llano County
- Leon County
- Lubbock County
- McCulloch County (Central Texas Master Gardeners)
- McLennan County
- Midland County (Permian Basin Master Gardeners)
- Milam County
- Montgomery County
- Nacogdoches County
- Palo Pinto County
- Parker County
- Randall County
- Rockwall County
- Rusk County
- San Patricio County
- Sterling County (Concho Valley Master Gardeners)
- Smith County
- Somervell County
- Tarrant County
- Taylor County
- Titus County (Cypress Basin Master Gardeners)
- Tom Green County (Concho Valley Master Gardeners)
- Travis County
- Victoria County
- Walker County Master Gardener Association
- Washington County (Bluebonnet Master Gardener Association)
- Wichita County
- Williamson County
- Wood County

GLOSSARY

Acid soil: A soil with a pH below 7.0. Also known as "sour" soil.

Alkaline soil: A soil with a pH above 7.0. Also known as "sweet" soil.

Astringent: Makes you pucker.

Bare root: Without soil, dug from the field, not container grown.

Bolt: Flower or seed stem formation.

Central leader: The main, upright, middle branch, or trunk of a tree.

Chlorosis: Yellowing of the foliage, often caused by an iron deficiency.

Clay: Heavy, "sticky" soil made up of very small, slippery particles.

Complete fertilizer: One that contains all three of the major nutrients essential for plant growth: nitrogen (N), phosphorus (P), and potassium (K).

Compost: Decomposed organic matter used for soil improvement and mulching.

Cover crop: Thick planting of a crop over the surface of a garden to reduce erosion, prevent weeds, and add organic matter.

Cross-pollination: Occurs when pollen is carried from one plant to another, usually by insects or wind.

Crown: Growing point above the root where the shoots and tops develop.

Deciduous: A tree or shrub that loses its leaves and is bare during the winter.

Diameter: The distance across the middle of a circle or through the middle of a tree, from one side to the other.

Exotic: Not native; introduced plants.

Germination: The first state in the growth of a plant from seed; sprouting.

Harden off: To accustom plants gradually to outside temperatures and conditions. Often used when transitioning indoor-grown transplants to outdoor conditions in spring.

Hardiness zones: Ten zones designated by the USDA across the country based on the average lowest temperatures. A zone's ranking helps determine whether a plant will survive the winter there.

Herbicide: A pesticide designed to kill or control weeds.

Inorganic: Generally refers to man-made chemical products not composed of animal or plant materials.

Insecticide: A pesticide designed to kill insects.

Leach: Loss of minerals due to water washing them out of the root zone.

Loam: A type of soil consisting of equal parts sand, silt, and clay. Generally ideal for growing fruits and vegetables.

Loppers: Long-handled pruners used for cutting woody branches.

Microclimate: A localized area with warmer or cooler temperatures than other areas close by.

Miticide: A pesticide designed to kill or control mites, usually spider mites.

Native: Indigenous to an area; has always grown there. Not exotic or introduced.

Nematode: A microscopic worm-like organism that attacks the roots of certain plants (especially tomatoes, figs, and okra), causing stunted and unhealthy growth.

Organic: A material composed of naturally occurring substances.

pH: A numeric scale for measuring the acidity or alkalinity of a soil ranging from 1 to 14. Acid soils have a pH of less than 7.0 while alkaline soils have a pH above 7.0 A soil with a pH of 7.0 is termed "neutral."

Sand: A well-drained, gritty soil composed of large soil particles.

Self-fruitful: Produces fruit without being cross-pollinated by another plant or variety.

Shatter: Occurs when spent (dead) petals or ripe seeds fall to the ground.

Side-dress: To add fertilizer on the soil surface beside plants so that light cultivation and watering move it into the root zone.

Silt: A friable (loose) soil with particles sized between those of silt and clay and with some characteristics of both.

Slips: Cuttings from a plant. Used to propagate sweet potatoes.

Taproot: A primary, deep, central root of a plant.

Virus: An ultramicroscopic organism that invades plant cells and causes irreversible damage. There is no cure for viruses. They can be spread from one plant to another by insects.

Water soluble: Fertilizer that can be dissolved in water and then applied to plants.

Water sprout: Vigorous, sappy shoots produced by the trunks or main branches trees. They are generally unwanted and should be removed.

RESOURCES

Vegetable Seeds

Baker Creek Heirloom Seeds
2278 Baker Creek Road
Mansfield, MO 65704
417-924-8917
www.rareseed.com

Seed Savers Exchange
3094 North Winn Road
Decorah, IA 52101-7776
563-382-5990
www.seedsavers.org

Territorial Seed Company
P.O. Box 158
Cottage Grove, OR 97424-0061
800-626-0866
www.territorialseed.com

Tomato Growers Supply Company
P.O. Box 60015
Fort Myers, FL 33906
888-478-7333
www.tomatogrowers.com

Totally Tomatoes
334 W. Stroud Street
Randolph, WI 53956
800-345-5977
www.totallytomato.com

Twilley Seed
121 Gary Road
Hodges, SC 29653
800-622-7333
www.twilleyseed.com

Willhite Seed Inc.
P.O. Box 23
Poolville, TX 76487
800-828-1840
http://www.willhiteseed.com

Fruit and Nut Trees and Plants

Bob Wells Nursery
17160 Lake Lorraine Road
Lindale, TX 75771
903-882-3550
www.bobwellsnursery.com

Womack Nursery Co.
2551 State Highway 6
DeLeon, TX 76444-6330
254-893-3400
Email: pecan@womacknursery.com
www.womacknursery.com

Disease Diagnostic Laboratory

Texas Plant Disease Diagnostic Laboratory
1500 Research Parkway, Suite A 130
Texas A&M University Research Park
College Station, TX 77845
979-845-8032
Email: plantclinic@ag.tamu.edu
www.plantclinic.tamu.edu

Soil andWater Testing

Soil, Water, and Forage Testing Laboratory
Department of Soil and Crop Sciences
AgriLIFE Extension, Texas A&M System
2478 TAMU
College Station, TX 77843-2478
979-845-4816
www.soiltesting.tamu.edu/

Stephen F. Austin State University
Soil, Plant, Water Analysis Laboratory
P.O. Box 13025
SFA Station
Nacogdoches, TX 75962-3025
936-468-4500
www.ag.sfasu.edu

Texas Gardening Magazines

Neil Sperry's Gardens
400 W. Louisiana
McKinney, TX 75069
800-752-4769
www.neilsperry.com

Texas Gardener
P.O. Box 9005
Waco, TX 76714-9968
800-727-9020
www.texasgardener.com

Gardening Information

Aggie Horticulture
Texas A&M Department of Horticultural Sciences
www.aggie-horticulture.tamu.edu

Jerry Parson's Plant Answers
www.plantanswers.com

SFA Gardens
Stephen F. Austin State University
Box 13000 SFA Station
Nacogdoches, TX 75962
936-468-1832
www.arboretum.sfasu.edu

PHOTOGRAPHY CREDITS

Cover Photography and Illustrations
Cool Springs Press would like to thank the following contributors to *Texas Fruit & Vegetable Gardening*.

Front Cover Main Image
Hot Pepper (*Capsicum annuum*), www.Thinkstock.com

Cover photography provided by Tom Eltzroth
Blueberries (*Vaccinium ashei*), Cabbage (*Brassica oleracea*) Carrots (*Daucus carota*), Corn (*Zea mays*), Potatoes (*Solanum tuberosum*), Strawberries (*Fragaria ananassa*), and Watermelon (*Citrullus lanatus*).

Interior Photography Credits
Dave Wilson Nursery: 183, 190; Ed Rode: 158; Felder Rushing: 171; Greg Grant: 8, 9, 12, 13, 15, 16, 17, 18, 19, 20, 21, 22, 24, 26, 27, 28, 29, 32, 34, 35, 36, 38, 39, 40, 41, 42, 43, 44, 49, 50, 51, 53, 55, 56, 58, 59, 60, 64, 77, 89, 98, 109, 110, 111, 115, 116, 123, 124, 127, 132, 134, 135, 137, 138, 142, 146, 147, 148, 149, 153, 156, 159, 165, 168, 174, 175, 179, 180, 181, 187, 198, 199, 200, 218, 219, 231, 232, 234, 237; Joe Lamp'l: 52; Liz Ball: 183; Lorenzo Gunn: 184, 194; Neil Soderstrom: 30, 31, 37, 45, 50; Robert Bowden/Leu Gardens: 176a, 176b; Tom Eltzroth: 62, 67, 69, 70, 73, 74, 78, 81, 82, 85, 86, 90, 93, 94, 97, 101, 102, 104, 105, 106, 112, 119, 130, 128, 131, 141, 150, 154, 160, 162, 166, 167, 170, 172, 188; Alamy: 190 © blickwinkel; Getty Images: 47, 48, 191, 193; iStockphoto.com/Mary Schowe: 14; iStockphoto.com/Michael Pettigrew: 46; iStockphoto.com/Kristen Johansen: 145; John Foxx/Stockbyte/Thinkstock: 157; Thinkstock: 61

BIBLIOGRAPHY

Growing Fruits, Berries, and Nuts in the South, George Ray McEachern, Pacesetter Press, 1978.

Heirloom Gardening in the South, William C. Welch and Greg Grant, Texas A&M University Press, 2011.

Knott's Handbook for Vegetable Growers, Oscar A. Lorenz and Donald N. Maynard, Wiley-Interscience, 1980.

The Lone Star Gardener's Book of Lists, William D. Adams and Lois Trigg Chaplin, Taylor Publishing, 2000.

Month-By-Month Gardening in Texas, Dan Gill and Dale Groom, Cool Springs Press, 2000.

Southern Herb Growing, Madalene Hill and Gwen Barclay, Shearer Publishing, 1987.

Texas Gardening Guide, Dale Groom, Revised Edition, Cool Springs Press, 2002.

Texas Gardener's Guide to Growing and Using Herbs, Diane Morey Sitton, Texas Gardener Press, 1987.

Texas Gardener's Resource, Dale Groom and Dan Gill, Cool Springs Press, 2009.

The Texas Lawn Guide, Steve Dobbs, Cool Springs Press, 2008.

The Texas Peach Handbook, Jim Kamas and Larry Stein, Texas A&M University Press, 2011.

The Texas Tomato Lover's Handbook, William D. Adams, Texas A&M University Press, 2011.

The Vegetable Book, Sam Cotner, Texas Gardener Press, 1985.

Vegetables, Delphine Hirasuna, Chronicle Books, 1985.

MY FAMILY RECIPES

GREG GRANT

BUTTERMILK CORNBREAD

Cornbread is, of course, an all-American classic in the South. My Papaw always said cornbread could outrun light bread any day of the week. I adapted this from a Southern cornbread recipe that originally called for "sweet milk." But, my Papaw drank lots of buttermilk and he was strong as an ox, so that's what we put in our cornbread.

1 cup stone-ground yellow cornmeal
1 cup all-purpose flour
2 teaspoons seasoned salt
1 teaspoon baking powder
1 teaspoon baking soda
1 teaspoon baking soda
2 tablespoons brown sugar
2 large eggs, beaten
½ cup vegetable oil
(bacon grease is even better!)
1 cup buttermilk

Preheat the oven to 350 degrees F. Cover the bottom of a cast-iron skillet with bacon grease or vegetable oil, and heat on the stovetop over medium-low heat. Mix the cornmeal, salt, baking, powder, baking soda, and brown sugar in a large bowl. Add the eggs, oil, and buttermilk and stir until blended. Sprinkle a bit of cornmeal into the hot skillet, then pour the batter into the skillet. Place the skillet in the oven and bake for 30 minutes or until the top is slightly brown and firm to the touch. Flip the cornbread onto a plate, then back onto a rack, top side up, to cool a bit and to prevent moisture from collecting on the bottom of the plate. Serve with real butter and anything from the garden.

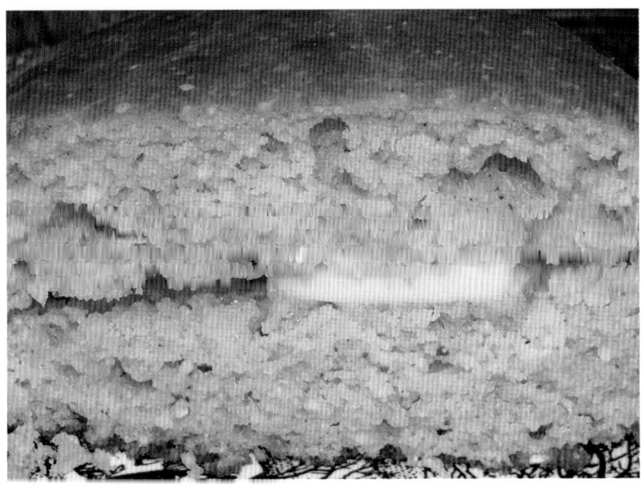

CHEWY PECAN PRALINES

This isn't the easiest recipe to make and it's quite time-consuming, but as they say, "Good things come to those who wait." I got this recipe from the Seguin-Guadalupe Valley Pecan Growers booth at the 1988 Folklife Festival in San Antonio. These pralines are somewhere between heavenly and divine. Sometimes I drizzle a bit of bittersweet chocolate (melted with a little paraffin wax) on them to keep my dad from eating them all, as he doesn't like chocolate. The recipe makes between 70 and 90 pralines, depending on how big you drop them.

2 cups sugar
2 cups light corn syrup
1 pound unsalted butter
2 cups whipping cream (not whipped)
2 teaspoons vanilla
7 to 8 cups chopped pecans (you can use as little as 5 cups)

Cook the sugar and corn syrup in a saucepan over medium-low heat until a candy thermometer reaches 250 degrees F. Remove from the heat, add the butter, and stir until the sugar is dissolved. Add the whipping cream slowly. Return the saucepan to the heat, stirring constantly. Cook until a candy thermometer reaches exactly 242 degrees F. This will take a while and you will get tired of stirring. Remove from the heat. Add the vanilla and pecans. Stir with your strongest arm until the mixture is cream colored and begins to stiffen. Drop by spoonfuls onto aluminum foil sprayed with vegetable oil spray. When the pralines are cool, wrap them in plastic wrap and hide them.

MICROWAVE PEANUT BRITTLE

I'm not fond of microwaves and don't even own one. But they sure are handy for heating up leftovers, melting butter, and making the once-difficult task of making peanut brittle easy. I got this recipe from Barbara Richardson's 1988 cookbook, *From My Kitchen.* Her son Jeff and I went to school together in Longview. He and I even played a saxophone (me) and trumpet (Jeff) rendition of "When the Saints Go Marching In" at the fifth-grade talent show at Mozelle Johnston Elementary School in Longview. Peanut brittle doesn't last very long around the Grant house, so you better show up right after it's made. You might have to adapt the cooking time to your microwave.

1 cup raw peanuts
1 cup sugar
½ cup light corn syrup
⅛ teaspoon salt
1 teaspoon butter
1 teaspoon baking soda

Mix the peanuts, sugar, syrup, and salt in a microwave-proof bowl (I use a large 2-quart Pyrex measuring bowl). Microwave on full power for 3 minutes. Stir. Microwave for 2½ minutes. Add the butter and microwave for 1 minute more. Add the baking soda and stir gently until the mixture is light and foamy. Quickly pour and spread the mixture onto a greased cookie sheet (I use vegetable oil spray). Let the peanut brittle cool and break it into pieces. The peanuts should smell like they are roasted, not burned, and the brittle should have a golden color. Eat all you can before anybody knows you made it.

SOUTHERN PEAS (OR ANY FRESH SHELL BEANS)

I grew up eating peas or beans with almost every meal. We generally had purple hull peas at everyday meals and cream peas on holidays. Always remember that fresh (or frozen) peas taste better than dried ones. Of course, I love butter beans as well and can't get enough. That reminds me of my favorite verse from an old folk tune (sung to the melody of "Just a Close Walk with Thee").

Who's that lady standing over there?
The one with the rollers all up in her hair.
She's not pregnant as she seems.
She just ate too many of them butter beans!

Cut salt pork (or bacon) into bite-size pieces and place in a large pot. Cook over medium heat for 15 minutes. Add a quart of water or enough to cover the peas or beans, and bring to nearly a boil. Add the peas or beans, simmer for a few minutes, and season with seasoned salt, garlic power, and pepper. Cook over low heat for at least 40 minutes or until the peas or beans are tender. They will taste even better if you put a lid on the pot and let them sit for 20 minutes before eating. This recipe works for purple hull, cream, and crowder peas as well as fresh pintos, butter beans, and limas.

DILL PICKLES

I've been growing cucumbers and dill so my mom can make dill pickles since I was a young boy. There's no telling how many quarts of pickles my family has eaten in our lifetime. She used to put up over one hundred quarts each year. You'd think the whole darned bunch of us was permanently pregnant! This recipe works equally well for pickled okra. It's also great for marinating cucumbers. Just pour the hot brine over the sliced fresh cucumbers, put them in the refrigerator overnight, and refrigerate what you don't eat. They have a great fresh flavor. My family loves these marinated cucumbers as much as (if not more than) the preserved ones.

For each sterilized 1-quart jar:
1 to 2 hot peppers
2 garlic cloves
1 head of fresh dill
1 grape leaf

Cucumbers and brine:
Small whole cucumbers
2 quarts water
4 cups apple cider vinegar
¾ cup rock salt

Place the hot peppers, garlic, dill, and grape leaf in each jar. Add the cucumbers. Heat the water, vinegar, and rock salt in a large pot until boiling. While the brine is hot, pour it over the cucumbers in the jars. Wipe the rims clean and place the lids on the jars. Put the jars into hot water and boil for 10 minutes. They will seal as they cool.

BREAD-AND-BUTTER PICKLES

My family has been a fan of homemade dill pickles for years. But lately we've all changed into bread-and-butter fans. I guess we get sweeter as we age. These pickles go with everything and have a flavor that brings back memories of eating at our grandparents' house in the country. My mom adds a grape leaf to each jar of pickles to help keep them crisp.

For each sterilized 1-quart jar
25 to 30 medium-sized cucumbers
1 head of cauliflower (optional)
4 large onions
2 large bell peppers
½ cup salt
5 cups apple cider vinegar

5 cups sugar
2 tablespoons mustard seeds
1 teaspoon turmeric
Grape leaves (1 per jar; my mom uses muscadine)

Slice the cucumbers and then break the cauliflower into pieces, if using. Coarsely chop the onions and peppers, and combine with the cucumbers and salt in a large bowl. Let the vegetables stand for 3 hours with ice on them. Drain. Combine the vinegar, sugar, mustard seeds, and turmeric in a large pot. Bring to a boil. Add the drained vegetables and heat thoroughly but do not boil. Put 1 grape leaf into each sterlized quart-sized jar, add the cucumber mixture, and seal.

SWEET POTATO CASSEROLE

My taste buds have always been confused by sweet potatoes. After all, are they a fruit or a vegetable? Are they supposed to be sweet or savory? I want them to be one way or the other, not hovering in between. When I eat baked sweet potatoes, I cover them with butter, seasoned salt, and pepper so I know they're a veggie. And although the dish is a Southern classic, I'm not a fan of candied yams. They are too sweet to be a vegetable but not sweet enough to be a dessert. Am I supposed to eat them after the meal but before the dessert? Although my mom serves this sweet potato casserole with her meals, it belongs in the dessert category as far as I'm concerned. That's when (and why) I eat it. My mom got the recipe from her best friend, Mary Beth Hagood. We can't live without it.

4 large sweet potatoes, peeled and cut into chunks (about 3 cups)
½ cup sugar
½ cup butter
2 eggs, beaten
⅓ cup milk
1 teaspoon vanilla

Topping:
⅓ cup melted butter
1 cup brown sugar
½ cup all-purpose flour
1 cup chopped pecans

Preheat the oven to 350 degrees F. Boil the potatoes in a large pot of water until tender and drain. Mash them in a large bowl and mix in the sugar, butter, eggs, milk, and vanilla. Transfer the potato mixture to a greased 9 x 13-inch baking dish. Mix the topping ingredients in a small bowl, and sprinkle on top of the potato mixture. Bake in the oven for 25 minutes. The casserole can be made ahead and frozen.

COLESLAW WITH CREAMY DRESSING

Cabbage is good (and good for you), but coleslaw is even better. Newly picked cabbages from the garden will taste sweeter and fresher than those for sale in the grocery store that have been in storage.

1 small head of cabbage (or half of 1 large head), shredded
½ cup shredded carrots

Dressing:
1 cup mayonnaise
2 tablespoons Thousand Island dressing
1 teaspoon oil and vinegar dressing (optional)
1 tablespoon sugar
1 tablespoon lemon juice
Salt and pepper to taste

Mix the cabbage and carrots in a large bowl. Mix the dressing ingredients in a small bowl until even and creamy. Pour the dressing over the cabbage mixture and mix until evenly coated. Chill overnight in the refrigerator and serve.
(I usually can't wait that long.)

STRAWBERRY SMOOTHIE

If you have trouble getting your children or grandchildren to eat fresh fruit, try this. You can make it with any fruit, fresh or frozen. If you use frozen fruit, the smoothie is cold and slushy when you drink it. If there's any left over, freeze it in Popsicle molds for later treats. If the finished product isn't sweet enough, add a little sugar and blend.

2 cups frozen strawberries
Whole, skim, or rice milk (enough to fill the blender until three-fourths full)
1 (14-ounce) can sweetened condensed milk
Sugar to taste (optional)

Place all the ingredients in a blender and blend until smooth. Drink and loosen your belt.

SWEET CANE BARBECUE SAUCE

Although my dad's a cattle rancher and Texas is a barbecued brisket state, I cling to my Southeastern roots and prefer pulled pork barbecue. I developed this recipe using my own homegrown ribbon cane syrup and mix the sauce lightly with the pork before serving. Of course, others like to drizzle the sauce on their sandwich before eating. You can substitute store-bought molasses or sorghum if you don't live near a sugar cane farmer like me.

½ cup apple cider vinegar
1 (6-ounce) can tomato paste
1 cup ribbon cane syrup
Dash of Tabasco sauce
Dash of garlic powder
Salt and pepper to taste

Mix all the ingredients in a small saucepan, heat, and stir until smooth. Store in the refrigerator.

FRIED OKRA

My mom knows how to fry. She can put a good batter on a shoe. I have nephews that won't eat any vegetable except her fried okra. They call it "country popcorn." My burgundy okra cooks up a little darker but is just as tasty. If you don't get near the front of the line at our house, you don't get any fried okra.

1 egg
½ cup buttermilk
1 quart okra, sliced
1 cup all-purpose flour
¼ cup cornmeal
Vegetable oil for frying
1 teaspoon seasoned salt
1 teaspoon pepper

Beat the egg with a fork in a bowl large enough to hold the okra. Stir in the buttermilk. Add the okra and stir to coat. Add the flour and cornmeal to the okra mixture and stir to coat the okra. Heat the oil in a frying pan until very hot, then add the battered okra, a small amount at a time. Fry over medium heat for about 15 minutes, but do not stir. After at least 15 minutes, gently turn the okra with a spatula. Continue to fry until golden brown. Remove the okra from the frying pan and add the seasoned salt and pepper. Stand in front of the line to make sure you get some.

WINTER

SPRING

SUMMER

FALL

INDEX

MEET GREG GRANT

Greg Grant is a horticulturist, conservationist, garden writer, and seventh-generation Texan from Arcadia, Texas. He is coauthor of *Heirloom Gardening in the South—Yesterday's Plants for Today's Gardens* (2011, Texas A&M Press), *In Greg's Garden—A Pineywoods Perspective on Gardening, Nature, and Family* (2010, Kindle ebook), *Home Landscaping—Texas* (2004), and *The Southern Heirloom Garden* (1995). He also writes the popular "In Greg's Garden" column for *Texas Gardener* magazine, contributes regularly to Neil Sperry's *Gardens* magazine, and writes a monthly gardening blog for Arbor Gate Nursery (www.aborgate.com). He serves as a part-time research associate for garden outreach at Stephen F. Austin State University's SFA Gardens in Nacogdoches, Texas.

Grant has degrees in floriculture and horticulture, both from Texas A&M University, and has attended post-graduate classes at Louisiana State University, North Carolina State University, and Stephen F. Austin State University. He has experience as a horticulturist with the Pineywoods Native Plant Center, Mercer Arboretum, San Antonio Botanical Gardens, and Texas Agricultural Extension Service, as an instructor at Stephen F. Austin University and Louisiana State University, and served on the staff of Naconiche Gardens and The Antique Rose Emporium.

Greg has introduced a number of successful plants to the Texas nursery industry, including the following: 'Blue Princess' verbena; dwarf pink Mexican petunia; 'Gold Star' esperanza; 'Laura Bush' and 'VIP' petunias; 'John Fanick' phlox; 'Stars and Stripes' pentas; 'Pam's Pink' honeysuckle; 'Lecompte', 'Salina's Pink', and 'Flora Ann' vitex; 'Henry Duelberg', 'Augusta Duelberg', and 'Rebel Child' salvias; 'Big Momma' and 'Pam Puryear' Turk's cap, 'Peppermint Flare' and 'Jackie Grant' hibiscus, and the 'Marie Daly' and 'Nacogdoches' (now called 'Grandma's Yellow') roses.

He was presented the Superior Service Award by the Texas Agricultural Extension Service and the Lynn Lowery Memorial Award by the Native Plant Society of Texas for horticultural achievement in the field of Texas native plants.

He has traveled extensively to hundreds of botanical gardens throughout the United States and Europe and has given more than one thousand entertaining and educational lectures. He is a graduate of the Benz School of Floral Design, a member of the Garden Writers Association of America, and a lifetime member of the Native Plant Society of Texas, the Big Thicket Association, the Texas Bluebird Society, and the Southern Garden History Society, where he serves on the board of directors. His garden, farm, and plant introductions have been featured in a number of magazines and newspapers, including *Texas Gardener*, *Texas Live*, *Woman's Day*, *Farm and Ranch News*, *The Daily Sentinel*, *The Dallas Morning News*, *San Antonio Express News*, and the *Houston Chronicle*.

Greg lives in deep East Texas in his grandparent's restored dogtrot farmhouse, where he tends terriers Rosie and Molly, a yard full of chickens, a patch of sugar cane, and more than one hundred bluebird houses.